What Others Are Saying About Jo Garner…

I needed a lot of help. I thank God for Jo. I was especially pleased. My family is in a beautiful home.

Ron Soldano

This book is going to help a lot of people. Until we met Jo, we thought there was no place to start. Jo helped us. She made it all about helping us.

John Flatman

Choosing the Best Mortgage – The Quickest Way to the Life You Want *is a great resource and an essential guide for real estate professionals and those interested in obtaining the best mortgage. She uses real-life stories in an informative and entertaining way.*

Jo Rook

CHOOSING THE BEST MORTGAGE

The Quickest Way to the Life You Want

JO GARNER

Henry Lyon Books
   in cooperation with Master Design Marketing, LLC
   789 State Route 94 E, Fulton, KY 42041
   HenryLyonBooks.com

ISBN Paperback: 978-1-947482-34-0
ISBN Ebook: 978-1-947482-35-7

Printed in the United States

10 9 8 7 6 5 4 3 2 1

I dedicate this book to my mother,
Janice Frizzell Garner.
She was a cheerleader in school and a cheerleader
in life, reminding me and others who crossed her
path to trust God, do our best, and that we could
accomplish anything we set our hearts to do.

Contents

Appendices

Preface

This book is meant to be educational in its purpose and not a solicitation for business in my capacity as a licensed mortgage officer. Mortgage lending rules and regulations change, so it is important to check for updated details on loan products and practices.

Acknowledgments

SOMEONE SAID THAT we become like the five people closest to us. If you want to be a person of excellence, choose your friends and associates wisely, and keep people of excellence in your closest circle of friends.

I want to thank the following people of excellence that have supported me in my career and the writing of this book.

Thank you to the bank and mortgage professionals throughout my career: teachers and role models reminding me that the mortgage business, like any business, is a people business. Most of these professionals already know who they are, but I can start with a few names from the long list with Linda Galigher, Linda Garrett, Jane Mazer, Pam Caviness, Jeff Sundling, Susan Belew...

Thank you to Lou Celli, who took me under his wing after my father passed away. Lou was head of the finance committee at the church where I was a member. Lou allowed me to serve as his assistant when he did budget counseling with families encountering hard times. Lou shared his time and knowledge as he helped these families develop financial habits and a better life.

Thank you to Terri Murphy, an author, national speaker, real estate and mortgage trainer, and coach. Terri was a role model for me when I became the radio talk show host for Real Estate Mortgage Shoppe. I consider Terri Murphy a mentor who has been a great support and a continued source of encouragement.

Thank you to Monica D'Amico, underwriting expert, for taking the time and attention to review our chapters on loan programs. Monica is a highly respected mortgage underwriter. Her insights and suggestions add much value to this book.

Thank you to the business friends at our business networking group at Talk Shoppe and BNI for encouraging me to pursue writing this book and keeping me accountable to stay on it until it was finished. Thanks, Peggy Lau, for the weekly accountability calls. Thank you to Mark van Stolk, Eric Eurich, and Donnie Tuttle for your game-changing business and sales coaching.

Last but certainly not least, thank you for the bedrock of support from my friends and family.

Introduction

THANK YOU FOR taking the time to pick up and read this book *Choosing the Right Mortgage – The Quickest Way to the Life You Want.* While reading this book, I hope you will seize upon the opportunity to move quickly into the life you want. This book is an informative and entertaining guide for real estate professionals, mortgage professionals, and other related industry professionals to use personally and share with customers and clients.

As a licensed mortgage loan officer, I get to be on my mortgage customer's journey to homeownership, or a positive life-changing refinance as their lender. Getting to walk alongside my mortgage clients this way is the thrill that keeps me excited to get up every day and go to work. The people-side of the financing business has kept me energized to stay in it for over 30 years.

These mortgage customers and referring partners have enriched my life experience and taught me so much. I love to share exciting and innovative ways my past mortgage customers have overcome barriers to living a better life. I am still sharing what I have learned with my current mortgage clients, and the stories you will experience in this book I have shared on the radio as host for Real Estate Mortgage Shoppe. Real Estate Mortgage Shoppe is broadcast over the airwaves in the Greater Memphis, Tennessee, geographical area on AM and FM channels, and across the internet. Now, I have the opportunity to share these financing tools and stories with you through this book.

The purpose of this book is to present to you valuable principles of how you can make the financing on your home support you in the pursuit of your life dreams. I will share stories and essential points about various mortgage products and situations to deepen your understanding of how you can use these financing tools to find your unique solutions.

For more resources, stories, and more, go to www.JoGarner.com. Let's stay connected!

CHAPTER 1

Knowing THIS Will Set the Course for Your Whole Life

You are only one decision away from a totally different life.
Anonymous

DEEP DOWN, WE all have gifts and talents that make us feel alive. As we enjoy using them, we come to love the very people who need what we have to give ... and the world becomes a better place.

When you follow your heart this way, your life purpose becomes clear. Doors open. People and resources are drawn to you. Like the early morning fog clearing as you drive higher up a hill, your "WHY" reveals itself to you.

What is your WHY?

After 30 years of serving as a mortgage loan officer, I still feel a thrill when someone invites me into their journey toward homeownership or achieving a financial milestone. Each person has a different story, a different struggle, a different kind of triumph ... and they all enrich my life.

It brings me great joy to learn all I can about the mortgage business, so I can remove barriers and smooth the way for my clients. Knowing that I helped another family get the best mortgage program on the best terms is my deepest satisfaction.

In this book, we'll learn from the lives of some of my hall-of-fame mortgage clients. These are individuals and families who wanted to make life better but ran into roadblocks. Necessity can truly be the mother of invention. Discover what creative solutions they successfully implemented to bring their dreams to life, and learn how they overcame the very obstacles you may be facing today. (Client names used throughout the book are fictitious.)

Mr. and Mrs. Flannery

A cycle of hardship continually pressed down on Mr. and Mrs. Flannery as it seemed everything from compromised health to losing their car prevented them from getting the better jobs ... and better pay ... they needed.

Mr. Flannery said, "Time after time, I would finally get up on my feet when something else would crash in on me and take me down again. It was like a terrible movie where you just want to click off the television but can't because the movie is about you, you are the onstage actor, and the film is still rolling."

The Bingham Family

Mr. and Mrs. Bingham had always worked hard, paid their bills on time, and were pleased with the way they handled their finances. Life was good ... until it wasn't.

One day, their daughter came home from college with recurring migraines that turned out to be a crippling illness. She was fighting for her life and needed her parents fighting with her. The Binghams took off work and poured everything into saving their daughter.

As though hit with a wave of cold water, the couple saw that they were headed toward bankruptcy.

How could they save their daughter without destroying their finances?

Zana Zager

Zana Zagar received both good news and bad news all in one day. The good news—the sellers accepted Zana's offer to buy the dream home she searched long and hard to find ... but they needed to close quickly. Zana would not have time to get her current home ready to sell before needing to close on the new one. The temporary bridge loan was the answer for Zana Zager. (See Chapter 14.)

Mr. and Mrs. Smith

Mr. and Mrs. Smith wanted their son to be able to go to college at their out-of-state *alma mater*, but the tuition plus living expenses would strain their budget.

Just how much would they be required to sacrifice to get their son to graduation?

Karen Kenner

Karen Kenner worked hard throughout her career. She had sacrificed to invest in her retirement and hoped to have her home paid off by then. Retirement loomed ahead and she realized with panic that all she had invested and saved would not be enough. Her expenses were still too high.

What financial tweaks could she make today to ensure more security and freedom tomorrow?

Opal Osborn

Her son called me and said, "My elderly mother lives alone and does not want to move into an assisted living facility. She loves living in her home, but she does not have the money to repair it and live there safely."

Joseph Jefford

Following a devastating divorce, Joseph said, "I love my kids. I want a house that I can make a home where they will love to come and spend time visiting with their dad."

Betty Bercoff

"My husband took care of the finances. When he suddenly died, it was up to me to survive on my own."

Bo Binkins

"I feel cramped in the city. I want to live in the country with a little farmhouse, fresh air, and a fish dangling at the end of my line."

Several times, Bo tried to get a loan approved for a house in the country. Over and over his attempts failed—either because the house he wanted needed too many repairs, his credit scores were too low, or he just didn't have the funds to cover closing costs. Bo felt hopeless.

Ricky (Mr. Fix-It)

"I want a house in the upper-priced neighborhood where some of my family lives, with a shop where I can make extra money working on cars."

How could Ricky accomplish this with neither the income to qualify for the mortgage in that price range nor the money for the down payment? Ricky engaged his ingenuity. He found a house in a neighborhood that was going steadily up in value, even though it wasn't the upscale area he initially wanted.

Over time he improved the garage and house. Property values were also rising. Ricky now had options. He could accomplish his original goal by selling his current home and taking the net profit from the sale of his home to put down on the more upscale new home, or he could keep his current home and rent it out as an income-producing property to help him make payments on the new home.

Barry

"I yearn to spend more time with my children and grandchildren. Where could I find investment money to purchase enough income-producing real estate so I can permanently quit my day job?"

Getting to Your WHY

A while back, I had a great sales coach. He taught me that once I fully grasped the "burning-in-your-gut reason" that compelled me to action towards my dream—my WHY — that WHY would empower my every effort.

"Then," he explained, "once you grasp your WHY, you need a clear vision. Your WHY and a clear vision will propel you with greater endurance."

In his book, *Start with Why,* Simon Sinek famously expounds how your compelling WHY will always move you further and faster than a goal.

To illustrate, Sinek compares Samuel Pierpoint Langley and the Wright Brothers. Does anyone remember Samuel Langley? Yet, most people recognize the names Orville and Wilbur Wright and what they invented.

Samuel Langley had substantial funding from the United States Government to invent the first manned flying machine. Langley also had a bevy of top brains from Harvard University to help him. *The New York Times* followed Langley and his team everywhere, giving him free publicity and plenty of notoriety. Langley, you would think, had all the key ingredients to success—funding, a brilliantly educated team, and the country's best marketing.

Orville and Wilbur Wright had no funding except the meager profits they eked out of their bicycle shop. They were not highly educated. National newspapers were not marketing them. They had every reason to fail—no funding, skilled team, or marketing; nevertheless, whom do we credit as the first to invent the airplane?

Unlike their competition from Langley's camp, the Wright brothers had a driving cause and a burning-in-the-gut desire to change the world's course by inventing the first manned flying machine. They were driven by such a strong WHY that they didn't need fancy funding, a team of engineers, or marketing. They worked with blood, sweat, and tears, day in and day out until they finally got the Wright Flyer airborne in Kitty Hawk, North Carolina, in 1903.

On the other hand, Langley was not compelled by a WHY. He merely had a *goal.* Langley and his team went to work every day for fame and a paycheck, not for a purpose.

The day it was announced that the Wright Brothers had invented the first motor-powered, manned airplane, Langley quit. He had a goal but not the WHY he needed to motivate him to overcome the obstacles.

The story of Langley and the Wright Brothers illustrates the difference between having a big WHY to fulfill a high purpose, or a small, self-centered goal … like being famous and making money.

Think about your WHY. It'll get you through any hard times on your way there. Then, once you know this vital reason for pursuing your dream, it'll be important to have a vision.

Getting a Sharp Focus on YOUR Vision

My sales coach told me the story of Diana Nyad, the first person known to swim from Cuba to Florida unaided. Diana attempted this several times and failed.

Once, a jellyfish attacked her. Another time, she tangled with aggressive sharks. However, most of her failures came from sheer fatigue.

During Diana's final attempt to swim from Cuba to Florida, she became exhausted, just like in times past. The difference on this occasion was her coach, who called her to attention from a nearby boat: "Look up at the light! Do you see that light ahead?"

Diana was so worn out, she could barely see the distant light and thought it a sunrise. Waving his arms emphatically her coach roared, "That light is on the Florida coastline! Don't give up, Diana! Keep swimming!"

Once Diana got a clear vision of the Florida coastline, adrenaline flooded her system and bolstered her forward with fresh vigor all the way to the finish. Diana Nyad was 64 years old when she became the first ever to claim this record-breaking swim.

Ask yourself:
- What do you want to achieve?
- Why?
- Who do you want to be as a person?
- Are your work and home life what you've dreamed they would be? How could they be better?
- Do you want children and friends in your home?
- Picture your ideal day. How do you feel? What do people say about you?

I challenge you to build a vision board for yourself. My retired US Navy friend, Peggy Lau, convinced me to make one, and they work.

Picture your home, business, and more. Use magazine cutouts or search for online photos. Find images representing the look and feel of your ideal life. Cut and paste the images onto your vision board. Put your vision board where you can see it every day ... and then watch what happens.

In my almost 30 years in the mortgage business I have seen real estate fortify a good life for my customers in countless ways. I believe that you can accomplish ANYTHING by owning real estate ... and if you buy it right, and keep buying more of it, the possibilities in what you can do in life for yourself and others become endless.

Questions to Answer before Choosing Your Mortgage

How much can you comfortably pay per month for a house note today? (See chapter on Budgeting.)

How much can you comfortably pay as a down payment today? (See chapter on Budgeting.)

How long do you plan to own the home that is being financed? Less than five years or more than five years?

General Rules of Thumb:

If more than five years: Choose a Fixed Rate mortgage with the lowest interest cost and the least mortgage insurance paid over time.

If less than five years:
- Choose a mortgage program with the least amount of closing costs.
- Choose a mortgage program with no pre-payment penalty.
- Compare a fixed rate with an adjustable variable interest rate mortgage program.

If you choose a variable rate loan product, you must have more than one possible profitable exit strategy. If the worst thing happened in the market, could you reallocate other investments to pay off the variable rate mortgage?

Drastic changes call for creative strategies. Do you see your financial situation drastically changing in less than five years?
- Retirement
- Inheritance
- Change in the number of household members
- Children going to college

- Divorce
- Downsizing
- Other
- None

Let's explore this more deeply.

Over the next 5 years:

— Are you receiving a large lump sum of money from a retirement plan or inheritance equal to twenty percent or more of the mortgage loan balance? (If no, skip to the next question.)

If yes, compare a fixed rate with an adjustable-rate mortgage that has rate caps using the worst-case scenario on interest rate movement over four years. Also, consider a "recast" vs. a refinance to save costs.

NOTE: Most adjustable-rate mortgage programs include annual and life-time safety caps restricting how far your mortgage interest rate can move over time. Each year the rate is scheduled to change, the principal and interest payment is re-amortized based on the unpaid balance over the remaining years of the mortgage term. We'll discuss this more in Chapter 9, "Adjustable Rate Programs."

— Are you planning to increase the number of dependents in your household OR to help your children through college? (If no, skip to the next question.)

If yes, consider ways to make room for the extra expenses and cover your family members' needs:

- Identify any dispensable debt and eliminate it.
- Explore up-front and monthly costs if you sold your current home and moved to a less expensive one.
- Explore the costs and monthly payments if you refinanced your current mortgage.

— How much could you save each month if you eliminated the high interest you are paying on some of your debt by adding these debts to one low interest refinance mortgage?

Consider using some of the monthly savings from the refinance to pay extra on principal and get the mortgage paid off sooner.

Ask yourself: How will the terms on this mortgage make me happy?

What barriers are blocking you from getting the financing terms you want?

- Credit
- Funds needed to close
- Qualified income
- Appraisal
- Other

(See chapters 15-18.)

— For how many years do you need to own the house to make it worth buying or refinancing?

What type of professionals do you need to help you make the best decisions? *(For more support on creating your best team of professionals, see link to "Advice from the Pros," provided under Resources at the end of this chapter.*

Mortgage Hall of Fame

The Smiths

Children Going to College: Pay for College … Get a Free House?

Remember the Smiths? They wanted their son to be able to attend college at their out-of-state *alma mater*. Considering tuition and living expenses, they wondered how much they might have to sacrifice to get their son to graduation.

It was not much at all, as a matter of fact.

Mr. and Mrs. Smith stepped out of the box and decided to buy a home close to the university where their son could live. He went on the loan with them as the owner-occupant, so the deal didn't cost much out of pocket. Even better, their son rented two of the rooms to other students whose rent more than covered the mortgage payment. Very clever for the Smiths! They made money each month and built equity as their son built his credit.

Lydia Lovelace

Facing Retirement with a "Home-Made" Solution

Lydia Lovelace called me with a dilemma:

"Should I stay or should I go?"

Instead of downsizing after retiring, Ms. Lovelace contemplated selling her house and inviting her daughter and son-in-law to co-sign on a larger home with a mother-in-law wing...

...but her daughter's family loved the old house. They loved its location, the land, the pond and woods out back, and its layout.

Ms. Lovelace called on a licensed contractor to assess the costs of adding a private living unit to her old house rather than selling it and buying a new one.

The family also looked at other homes. They got estimates on monthly mortgage payments and money down for homes with comparable layout and location perks, like proximity to shopping and doctor's offices. After comparing these numbers to remodeling costs, they decided to modify the home instead of moving.

To pay for the remodel, the family considered two options: a cash-out refinance with a brand new fixed-rate first mortgage; or an interest-only, variable rate home equity line of credit. The Lovelace's decided on a fixed rate cash out refinance of the first mortgage to avoid the chance of interest rates taking the cost of the home equity line of credit up beyond their means.

The Bingham Family

"Blending" Debt

Mr. and Mrs. Bingham had excellent credit and always paid their bills on time. They felt good about their handling of finances over the years.

Then, their daughter came home from college with recurring migraines that turned out to be a crippling illness.

To be with her, the Binghams took time off from their jobs. While their income slowed to a trickle, monthly debts and expenses mounted. Mrs. Bingham took a leave of absence from her job.

Focused on saving their daughter's life, the Binghams figured on borrowing "just a little here and there" to make it. Over the course of

24 months, they racked up credit card debt beyond their ability to pay. Eventually, they were forced to dip into savings. After a while, as the debt snowballed, even that wasn't enough. A day was fast coming when they would have to choose between paying the mortgage or paying the credit cards.

Family and church friends tried to help, but that didn't cut it. Bankruptcy was in view. That's when their banker contacted me and asked if I could explore some mortgage options with them.

The Binghams sat across the desk from me with all their financial information, and I am glad to report that I knew then: there was still hope! They had quite a bit of equity in their house. They had money in their retirement funds. Now, it was time to think critically.

Exploring the options, we discovered the best solution: quickly refinance their current mortgage. Even with a higher rate, this fast action would save them substantially in the immediate and long-term future.

Here's what that looked like. *Rates and numbers represent the market rate at the time this story took place.*

House Value at the time of meeting $217,000
Original Mortgage (20-year term) $140,000
Amount Owed $100,000
Monthly P&I (7%) $1,085
Credit Card Debt 1 $20,000 at 15%
  Monthly minimum payment...$600
Credit Card Debt 2 $10,000 at 14%
  Monthly minimum payment $300
Total monthly payments $1,985

Solution:

Although the Binghams were on the brink of delinquency, this would have been their first time making a late payment. In the nick of time, they applied and got approved for a refinance.

The loan that worked for them looked something like this:
House Value...$217,000
New Mortgage (30-year term, New fixed rate 8%) ....~$137,000
New Monthly P&I (8%) $1,005

Savings:

The new loan replaced the $1,085 on the old loan. The credit card debt was added and factored into the new mortgage, eliminating the $600 and $300 revolving credit payments. The new loan covered closing costs and paid some taxes and insurance, too.

Old Debt and Monthly Payments ......$1,085 + $600 + $300 = $1,985
Monthly Payments on Old Debt...$1,005
Savings ....$1,985 – $1,005 = $980/month

Recapture formula based on payment savings: $4,000 closing costs /$980 monthly savings = 4 months cost recapture time

As their daughter's health improved, Mrs. Bingham was able to go back to work and increase their cash flow.

After the initial emergency, we weren't done!

Stage two goal was to begin allocating some of the Binghams' monthly savings towards extra principal payments so they could pay off their mortgage in 15 years or less. Over time, both their daughter's health and the Binghams' finances dramatically improved.

Sheree Shinolt

The Adventurous Life

Let me introduce you to Sheree Shinolt. At a young age, Sheree promised herself that she would prioritize experiencing life to the fullest over just making a lot of money.

After college, Sheree moved back into the bonus room at her parents' house. This enabled her to save money and bought her time to continue to "find herself" while establishing her career.

Sheree and a close group of friends took some memorable vacations to see the world, and she was still able to save money. She knew, though, that simply saving was not going to be enough. To live her life the way she envisioned, Sheree would need to invest and build her wealth over time. She realized there was nothing that could build the wealth she wanted like owning her own home.

Two years later, Sheree was excelling in her hi-tech career and it looked like she might be getting married. She reasoned that buying a home and locking in a 30-year fixed-rate mortgage would be much better than paying rent, which increases whenever a landlord decides, and which offers no financial return. Eventually, she would enjoy more discretionary money as her income increased and the P&I stayed the same.

She would also be building equity. What cash remained after expenses could go to the vacations and adventures yet on her bucket list.

It was finally high time for home ownership, which she believed would provide a launching pad to build wealth for herself and her future family ... but she got a small case of cold feet. How could Sheree, an adventuress whose whole life was yet before her, make a 30-year commitment to something so binding as a mortgage?

That's why Sheree and I went over several questions before even touching her application. I wanted her to consider not just the numbers, but the *emotional* payoffs of making this investment. If you can relate at all with Sheree's story, I encourage you to consider these questions, too.

- What benefits will I enjoy by owning a house?
- What disadvantages will I have to overcome?
- Are there any creative solutions that would get me equal or greater benefits with fewer disadvantages?
- How long do I plan to live in this geographical area?
- If I bought a home and then needed to move out of the area, what exit strategies would be available to me?

Sheree had firmly established in her mind the purpose—the strong WHY—for wanting to buy a house and get the right financing. At last, Sheree bought her own home and locked in the fixed interest rate mortgage. Sheree had taken the first exciting step toward many vacations and adventures to come.

Resources

"Get-It-Right-the-First-Time Mortgage Checklist" in Appendix 1

The Success Principles: How to Get from Where You Are to Where You Want to Be,
by Jack Canfield with Janet Switzer

Start with Why, by Simon Sinek

Visit **www.JoGarner.com** and navigate to "Advice from the Pros" for assistance building your expert team of professionals to help you make the best decisions.

CHAPTER 2

Determining How Fast You Can Recapture Your Loan Costs

You know you are getting old when the candles cost more than the cake.

Bob Hope

Cost Components to Consider

HAVE YOU EVER heard that "there is no such thing as a free lunch?" This old saying is true because even if you did not pay for it, someone paid for it on your behalf. The food cost something to produce, so it costs something to obtain. If you accept your free lunch and decide to stay for the evening meal with caviar, you should expect to pay extra, right?

When you get a mortgage equal to the current market rate, you may get a quote from the lender that lists the costs to consider:

- down payment
- closing costs
- property taxes
- insurance

To lock in a below-market rate, the lender would need to charge an extra fee to cover the extra cost of acquiring it. Lenders refer to this extra fee to buy down the interest rate as "points." One point equals 1% of the loan balance. Paying a full point can drop the mortgage in 0.25% increments; thus, lowering your monthly mortgage payment.

15

When you buy a home with a mortgage, there are three basic components to your costs.

First, most loan products require that you make a down payment. The minimum amount down varies with the loan product. The down payment is the difference between the sale price and the base loan amount.

Example:

Sale price	$100,000
Minimum Down for Conventional 5%	$ 5,000
Loan Amount	$ 95,000

Second, the closing costs include any processing or underwriting fees from the mortgage company, appraiser, credit agency, title company, county records office, state taxes for most states, and other third-party fees.

Third, most lenders require that you pay property taxes and homeowners insurance directly, while others require that you pay your property taxes and homeowners insurance into an escrow account. Either way, taxes and insurance must be paid at closing.

Most mortgage programs allow the seller of the property to pay up to a certain amount toward the borrower's closing costs if they negotiate these terms in the home purchase contract. This can include prepaid taxes and insurance, but the seller may *not* contribute to the down payment.

Example (buyer):

Sale price	$200,000
Down payment	$ 7,000
Closing costs	$ 4,000
Prepaid Taxes and Insurance	$ 3,000
Extra points to buy lower rate	$ 1,000
Total costs	$ 15,000

On an FHA loan, the seller is allowed to pay up to 6% of the sale price— OR—a portion of the closing costs including points and prepaid taxes and insurance MINUS down payment, whichever is less.

Example (seller):

6% Sale price	$200,000 x 6% = $12,000
Total MINUS Down Payment	$15,000 – $7,000 = $8,000

Since the latter option is lower than paying 6%, this seller could only pay up to $8,000 towards closing costs.

Homebuyers can still get into a home with zero to minimal move-in costs depending on the mortgage product.

The zero-down mortgage products usually have other restrictions borrowers must meet. For instance, the Veteran Administration Mortgage allows qualified veterans to get a mortgage with no down payment. The veteran may still negotiate closing costs and prepaid taxes and insurance with the seller. The USDA Rural Housing loan does not require a down payment if the property is in an approved area and the borrower meets certain qualifications, but remember: there is no such thing as a "free lunch." *Someone* still has to pay closing costs plus prepaid taxes and insurance.

The fees for getting a mortgage can vary from one lender to another. These costs can also vary from one mortgage product to another and can depend on the price of the mortgage rate in the market on any given day.

If you are borrowing $100,000 and paying 1% for the lender fee, the $1,000 fee goes towards the mortgage company's overhead including their lease, utilities, office supplies, and the loan officer's commission.

Suppose you purchase a rate that is priced 1% above its wholesale cost. In that case, the mortgage company does not have to charge the full lending fee of $1,000 because the higher-than-market interest rate compensates the lender when they later sell the income stream or the loan. The extra money the lender gets from the agency funding the loan is called a "lender premium." This lender premium can be applied to cover some of the buyer's costs.

Determined to Get Her Dream Home

Ms. Dominguez

This story is about a creative, determined mother who was short on funds but not on strategy to get the house of her dreams for her family.

A single mother of two children, Ms. Dominguez had driven past the cutest little house every day on her way to work. She adored this house, even sometimes visualizing her girls swinging on the swing set in the yard.

One day, the house went up for sale. Houses were selling fast in that neighborhood. At the same time, her apartment lease was soon up for renewal and the landlord was again ratcheting up the rent, which she was already struggling to pay.

If only she could find a way to buy that house.

She had savings to cover a down payment … but where would she get the funds to close?

We tried the USDA 100% loan, but the house was just outside the designated area, so it didn't qualify. The sellers had plenty of offers and preferred not to help with her closing costs or prepaid taxes and insurance. Ms. Dominguez tried not to lose heart.

She decided to settle for a higher mortgage rate and a slightly higher note. She tapped into savings to cover down payment. Then, she offered about $4,000 more than the sale price and requested the sellers use the extra $4,000 toward prepaid taxes and insurance and closing costs.

Ms. Dominguez locked in a mortgage interest rate that was about a half-point higher than the market rate, giving the lender an extra $3,000 as a lender premium to cover the rest of the closing costs. This was a win/win for both seller and buyer.

The day when Ms. Dominguez and her girls closed and got the keys to their new home was a day of true victory and celebration!

Ms. Dominguez home purchase transaction:

Seller asking price	$195,000
Sale price paid by buyer	$199,000
Down payment	$ 7,000
Closing costs	$ 4,000
Prepaid taxes and insurance	$ 3,000
Total	$ 14,000
Contract negotiated for seller to pay $4K since buyer paid $4K more for home (Lender premium of $3K paid for buyer's costs)	$ 4,000
Buyer's move-in costs	$ 7,000

The lender paid $3,000 toward buyer's costs because the buyer paid a rate higher than market. The mortgage company paid the $3,000 extra money—(lender premium) they got from the agency funding the loan toward Ms. Dominguez's costs.

Discount points can be purchased to lower your interest rate *below* the market rate. Each discount point costs 1% of the mortgage loan amount.

When the borrower pays points, he pays an advance lump sum towards interest to enjoy a lower rate and monthly payment.

How Points Work

If the market rate is 6% with a 1% origination fee, but you want a rate of 5.75%, you will need to purchase points to get the lower rate.

If 5.75% is priced one percent below the "wholesale" market price, then you would pay a 1% origination fee and 1% discount. The rates for some companies (not current rates in today's market) appear as follows:

- 5.75% 1+1 indicates that this rate is below market. The lender needs to charge their processing and underwriting fee *plus* enough to pay the rate's wholesale price and the cost to reduce the rate.
- 6% 1+0 indicates below wholesale rate and lender needs to charge their processing and underwriting fees.
- 6.25% 0+0 market rate (par)

If a borrower's income is too low to qualify for the loan amount she really wants, she might be willing to purchase an extra discount point to "buy down the rate," thus reducing her payment enough to qualify for the mortgage program.

When should you pay points? The best way to decide whether to pay points is to perform this simple break-even analysis:

- Calculate the cost of the points. For instance, if you borrow $100,000 on a 30-year loan at the market rate of 6% with a 1% origination fee and zero discount points, then the 1% origination fee will cost you $1,000. Your principal and interest payment will be $600 per month.

- Calculate the principal and interest payment for $100,000 over 30 years on a 6.25% rate with no origination fee and no discount points. Your principal and interest payment would be $616 per month. The difference between the two payments is $16.00 per month.

- Divide the cost of the origination fee ($1,000) by the amount of savings ($16.00) to determine how many months it will take you to break even on your investment. $1,000/$16.00 = 62.5 months or 5.2 years. The best investment would be the higher rate with no origination fee unless you plan to keep the house and the mortgage for over 5 years.

Refinance — How to Calculate How Fast You Can Recapture Your Closing Cost Investment

Hindsight is not a strategy.

Jane Bryant Quinn

How do you know whether refinancing is the right thing to do? Answer the following questions up front:

A.   How long do I plan to keep this home?

If you plan to keep the house for over five years and will enjoy substantial monthly savings on the new payment—OR—you will save enough in principle reduction over the time you plan to keep the house, then refinancing will be a positive move for you.

A simple way to see what you're saving over the life of the loan or just over the next few years is to compare the amortization schedules of your current and potential new loans. Compare long term interest payout, and how much you will pay out of pocket on monthly principal and interest.

B.   How fast can I recapture my closing costs?
The answer largely depends on you and your financial goals but aim to recapture your closing costs in 18-24 months maximum if you plan to be in the house five years or more.

Strategy 1: Lengthen the Mortgage Term

Karen Kenner

Karen Kenner had worked hard throughout her career. She sacrificed to invest in her retirement funds and hoped to have her home paid off by the time she retired. As retirement drew near, Karen grew anxious, as she was far from done with her mortgage loan and feared her bills were set to outweigh her retirement income.

Karen told me, "It suddenly hit me that I do NOT have to pay off the house. If I can refinance my mortgage back to a 30-year term on a rate below what I am currently paying for the 15-year loan, I can do more and live better with a smaller monthly payment and increased cash flow."

Karen was able to refinance back to a 30-year mortgage saving over $400 per month, which she allocated to paying additional principal until retirement. After retirement, she planned to put the extra $400 monthly into a savings plan for emergencies.

For Karen, this was the perfect solution to win back her peace of mind ... to help her sleep much better every night knowing her retirement years would be covered.

Refinancing to a lower rate and reducing the payment, as Karen Kenner did, is a common refinance solution.

If this strategy sounds good to you, then to calculate time to recoup your costs, take the cost you are paying to refinance and divide it by the dollar amount you are saving per month. For example, if the cost to refinance is around $4,000 and you are saving $400/month, it will take you ten months to break even or earn back the refinance cost.

So ... $400 monthly savings × 10 months = $4,000 recaptured.

Note to the wise: Be wary of refinancing offers touting "no closing costs." In many cases, you will pay thousands of dollars more over time with a higher interest rate.

Also for the wise: if you consider refinancing your existing mortgage to a lower rate, but you owe less than ten years on it, you may not be saving very much money. Check to see how much of your monthly payment is going toward principal compared to the amount going to interest. If almost the whole payment is allotted to paying the principal, you have already paid the interest portion of your mortgage. Refinancing to a lower interest rate for the sole reason of saving interest will not work, because you have already paid almost all of the interest.

Strategy 2: Shorten the Mortgage Term

The Rushings

Starting out, the Rushings were trying to pay off debt without much in the bank. They paid about 3.5% of the home price for a down payment. To give them some breathing room on their house payment, Rubin and his wife chose a 30-year fixed-rate mortgage. The low 30-year payment allowed them to build up some savings while paying down more debt.

Fast forward five years....

My phone rang.

"A voice from the past," he said joyfully, clearly happy about something. Rubin Rushing went on to share with me their story.

After buying their first home, Rubin and Rosie enrolled in the Dave Ramsey "get out of debt" program. They'd learned some clever methods of living a fun-filled life with their young children on a limited budget. When they got raises at work, they continued paying off debt and investing more and more money into an emergency fund.

Rubin described their plan to refinance their 30-year mortgage to a 15-year mortgage for a lower rate and to eliminate ten years (120 payments). Here's how they won their bragging rights:

The Rushings initially had a mortgage for about $172,000 on a 4.625% 30-year mortgage with an $884.32 principal and interest (P&I) payment, plus taxes and insurance, and FHA monthly mortgage insurance of about $119/month—a total of about $1,368/month.

- They refinanced their mortgage to a 15-year term …
- This lowered their rate a whole point. Their P&I payment increased by $246/month but …
- They eliminated the FHA mortgage insurance and lowered the interest over the whole loan amount for the entire term of the mortgage.

If the Rushings had not refinanced, they would have paid $884 P&I for the remaining 25 years for a total of $265,200 plus monthly FHA mortgage insurance. Since they refinanced, total P&I payments over the new 15-year term would come to $203,400 for a whopping savings of ~$61,680 plus the reduction in FHA monthly mortgage insurance costs. BRAGGING RIGHTS!

When considering a refinance to lower the rate and shorten the term, run two amortization schedules side-by-side.

The first amortization schedule is for the unpaid balance of your current loan with current interest rate and years remaining on the loan.

The second amortization schedule is for the refinance—new loan balance, new lower rate, and new term of the loan.

Calculate the interest on both to determine how much you will pay over the course of each loan.

Example:

When comparing the old loan amortization schedule, start with your current year on the mortgage (beginning year six in our example below). Calculate interest payments for the next five, eight, or ten years.

To see how much interest you will have paid, calculate the difference between today's balance and the balance in five, eight, or ten years.

Amortization schedule on current loan. The first five years were already paid, so we'll begin with year six.

	Principal	Interest	Principal + Int	Balance
Year 6	$278.88	$605.44	$884	$156,807

The estimate for the Rushings keeping their 30-year FHA loan with a P&I payment of $884 for the remaining 25 years (300 months) comes to about $265,200 plus FHA monthly mortgage insurance.

Amortization schedule on new 15-year refinance (original balance of $156,807 plus refinance closing costs and prepaid taxes and insurance).

	Principal	Interest	Principal + Int	Balance
Year 1	$689.84	$475.42	$1,165	$162,310

Total payments at end of this 15-year loan would be approximately $209,700. No FHA monthly mortgage insurance premium since new loan was a conventional loan product. Total payments on refinanced loan: $1,165 × 180 payments (15 years) = $209,700.

When the Rushings refinanced to a conventional loan with no monthly mortgage insurance, their payments would look something like this:

$689.84 + $475.42 = $1,165 P&I × 15 years (180 months) = $209,671

Total savings on refinance:

Old loan costs $265,200
MINUS Refinance loan costs $209,700
PLUS closing costs on the refinance $4,000
Total savings...$55,900

Plus they eliminated of FHA mortgage insurance!

Refinancing vs. Recasting

Edward and Elisa Eldridge

Edward and Elisa Eldridge had both lost their former spouses to cancer. Edward had lived alone in the same home for over twenty years, and Elisa did the same in her home for over ten. They both thought their chance of finding love again was one-in-a-million.

When I came into contact with Edward and Elisa, they shared the serendipitous story of how they met and fell in love. They got married and wanted to start a new life in a new home, but weren't ready to sell their current houses.

Elisa said, "It's like putting the cart before the horse. Once I sell my house and Edward sells his, we could use our profits to pay 50% as a down payment and enjoy a low house note ... but if we're not ready to sell our houses, where else could we get the same money?"

There are a number of ways Edward and Elisa could get the funds they wanted.

They could talk with a lender about an equity line of credit on their current homes. With more than $100,000 equity in both of their houses, the equity line would give them the $200,000 they wanted to pay down on the new house.

Another option would be to make a small down payment on the new home and aggressively pay it down. They would pay higher monthly P&I for a while on the new home until they were ready to sell their previous two houses.

They decided they wanted to pay the new mortgage down.

Since Mr. and Ms. Eldridge were paying well over 50% of the unpaid balance on their new mortgage as a prepayment to lower the loan balance, they had three options.

Option 1: Refinance for a lower payment on a brand new loan. They would have to pay some closing costs or roll the costs into the loan and they would have to lock in whatever mortgage rates were available at the time of the refinance.

Option 2: Refinance to shorten the mortgage term and pay it down faster.

Option 3: Request a "recast" instead of a refinance. When a borrower makes a prepayment to principal over 20% of the balance owed on the loan, that borrower can ask their lender to recast the payment to a lower amount reflecting the lowered balance, keeping the same rate they locked in when they originated the loan.

Lenders have the option to say yes or no to this request. The recasting of your payment to a lower amount would make it as if you never borrowed the larger loan amount. After you make the large lump sum prepayment to lower your mortgage principal balance, a recast re-amortizes the payment as if you never had the original, larger loan amount. You keep the interest rate but get a new monthly payment schedule. It is up to the lender to decide if they will agree to recast.

While the Eldridge's were comparing the recast to the refinance, the mortgage market improved and the Eldridge's moved forward with a full refinance to a much lower mortgage rate, giving them an even bigger savings.

Betty Bercoff

"My husband took care of the finances. When he suddenly died, it was up to me to survive on my own."

Life was good for Betty Bercoff and her husband. They trekked through their routine of going to work, coming home to share about their day over dinner. They enjoyed time with their friends and neighbors who would come to visit. The Bercoffs had downsized to a smaller home with less to clean and repair, and a little low maintenance landscaping to eliminate the back-breaking yard work of their previous years.

Betty's husband took care of the finances, and Betty took care of the cleaning, cooking, and making their house a home.

When Betty's husband suddenly passed away, she was plunged into a world utterly foreign to her. She still worked her job. She got help from friends … and she began taking stock of her financial situation. Her husband had left her with a small life insurance policy that did *not* pay off the mortgage, but it did give her time to make a budget and rearrange her spending habits.

Just as it looked like smoother roads were ahead, the Great Recession hit … and she lost her job. Even after finding a part-time job, the income was small. Her heart ached for her husband to be there to help her. She felt like a failure when she had to declare bankruptcy, but at least she was able to save her house.

Betty Bercoff was not a quitter. She knew she was a survivor. She got a second job and, over time, rebuilt her credit. She and her little dog Barkley were living sparsely but making it. Then the heating system went out in her house. The repairman told her it would cost her about $8,000 to replace it, requiring a home improvement loan that would *crush* her budget. That is when she called me to see if she could do a cash-out refinance to pay for the heat to be fixed.

"It takes less than 30 days to close a cash-out refinance," I told her.

Unfortunately, it was already winter and too cold to wait that long. Betty took the home improvement loan with the whopping big payment. Meanwhile, she and I worked together to get approval for her cash-out refinance with the home improvement loan added to the refinance loan.

Because of the amount she had already paid down on the existing mortgage and the lower interest rate she got on the refinance, her new payment with the two loans together was LESS than what she had been paying before. Betty not only survived this setback, but she also TRIUMPHED.

CHAPTER 3

Budget

GETTING TO THE TRUTH—
YOUR NET INCOME AND ASSETS

The simplest definition of a budget is "telling your money where to go."

Tsh Oxenreider

IT'S NOT AS **hard as you think...**

1. **Keep your mortgage payment low to leave room for the expenses that naturally expand and contract with life events.** On the radio show that I host, *Real Estate Mortgage Shoppe,*[1] I've had the privilege of talking with some of the best personal finance gurus, who suggest limiting your monthly house note to 25% or a maximum 30% of your gross income. Adding in other debts, taxes, insurance, and association fees, total debt should not exceed 38% to 41% of your gross income.

2. **Watch out for the automated underwriting systems.** They sometimes approve a mortgage for a lot higher debt. Before you apply, know your limit and don't compromise.

---

[1] Jo Garner hosts *Real Estate Mortgage Shoppe*, a radio show that has been airing from 2011 to the time of this writing on News Radio AM 600 WREC and 92.1 FM in Memphis, TN, and on iHeart Radio across the internet. Podcasts and show notes on www.JoGarner.com.

3. **Keep Emergency Funds as fuel to power through the unexpected.** The best brains in personal finance strongly suggest you keep an emergency fund. The general consensus is to keep a minimum three to six months of living expenses if you have a stable job with regular pay; or, one full year of living expenses for the self-employed. *Read more about this and other real estate and financial matters at the Real Estate Mortgage Shoppe.*

4. **Get to the truth about your income and expenses.**

The head of the finance team at our church was affectionately called *Baaba Lou.* We called him that because he and his wife served in a school in Zambia for a number of years, and the children called him *Baaba,* meaning "father."

Lou was brilliant at budget counseling because he and his wife had already lived it. They obtained excellent wealth just by practicing what he preached. It was a joy and privilege working under Lou Celli, serving those families who found themselves spending more than they earned either because of loss of work, medical expenses, or legal bills. Here are some easy steps Lou suggested to get on track with your budget.

Step 1: **Set a timer for one or two hours and hit play on your favorite tunes.** Commit to spending every minute of this time going methodically through each bank and credit card statement.

If you dread the task of budgeting, at least you know the pain will be over in two hours and you can enjoy listening to your favorite songs while you complete the task.

If going through all of the last 12 months causes a mental and emotional block, go for the last six or no less than three months of transactions.

Step 2: **Assign a category for each expense.** As you record the dollar amount, label it with an appropriate category such as monthly utilities, food, gasoline, internet/cable, mortgage, car payment, entertainment, business expenses, and so on. Also include bills you pay less frequently like car tags, property taxes, homeowners insurance, and so on.

TIP: There are many templates you can download and use for free to get you started, such as this one from moneyunder30.com/free-budget-spreadsheet.

december

▲ A	B	C	D	E	F	G	H	I
4								
5	december	groceries	electricity	gas	parking	dining out	charity	misc.
6	1							
7	2							
8	3							
9	4							
10	5							
11	6							
12	7							
13	8							
14	9							
15	10							
16	11							
17	12							
18	13							
19	14							
20	15							

Step 3: **Tally all expenses.** Now is also a good time to examine each item. Where can you cut back?

Step 4: **Determine your true income from pay stubs and bank deposits.** Be sure and record your **net** income. To calculate net, look at your latest pay stubs and itemize the deductions such as taxes, FICA, insurance, etc. Subtract all deductions from the gross amount to calculate what finally makes it to your back account, i.e., net income.

Step 5: **Ask for discounts.** Call companies and see if you can get a discount on their products or services.

One client succeeded at negotiating a much lower interest rate on his credit cards. He socked away quite a bit of savings just from this one step! *You have not because you ask not.* Why not ask?

Step 6: **Replace higher cost items with comparable lower costs items.** When shopping and dining, don't be afraid to ask questions.

Lou had a list of places where families could get great bargains. One on his list was my favorite grocery store. I found out from Lou that at 6 am they offered 75% off meat getting close to the sell-by date. A 75% reduction in meat costs could change your life … leaving 75% more "change" in your pocket.

Lou also taught me to find budget items that could be replaced with something similar but less costly. For example, if you love having pizza delivered to the house once a week for you and the kids, try buying some great frozen pizzas from the grocery store. Throw them in the oven while you are busy around the house or, even better, while you're resting. Pizza is ready in 15 to 20 minutes and you paid a lot less for heating them in *your* oven than having them delivered from someone else's.

Step 7: **Look for ways to increase your household income.** Work a second job when possible. Sell items you don't need. Find ways to make your home pay for itself.

Step 8: **Determine your comfort level on a house payment.** Now that you know your *true* income and *true* expenses, what can you comfortably afford to pay on a house note?

"Housing Ratio" is the monthly mortgage payment divided by gross income. "Debt-to-income ratio" (DTI) is the percentage of your gross monthly income that goes to paying your monthly debt payments including your proposed mortgage payment.

Determining Housing Ratio and DTI

Gross Income before taxes: $5,000/month

House payment assuming rate of 4.5% fixed for 30 years

+ $963 P&I
+ $100 estimated homeowners insurance
+ $225 estimated property taxes
+ $54 estimated temporary monthly private mortgage insurance
= $1,342/month paid to the mortgage company
+ $50 neighborhood association fee paid to neighborhood fund
= $1,392 total housing debt per month
  $1,392/$5,000= 27.84% housing ratio
+ $300/month car payment
+ $25/month minimum required credit card payment
+ $1,392 proposed housing debt per month
= $1,717/$5,000= 34.34 d debt-to-income ratio as calculated by the mortgage company
+ $1,500/month Federal taxes, FICA, and other payroll deductions from gross income
+ $900/month food, gasoline, cable and internet, services and other insurances, clothing, and other household items
= $4,117/month total costs subtracted from gross income leaves approximately $883 for charity, personal savings, and discretionary items.

Adding Income to the Budget with Rent

A House That Pays YOU

My house - A little cleanup and an extra room pay dividends.

When I first got into the mortgage business, money was short, but I understood the power of the fixed-rate mortgage to shelter my income by avoiding landlords' ever-increasing rent.

Necessity being the mother of invention, I was quick to think outside the box and set out to buy a house.

I found a realtor who knew what I wanted, where I wanted to live, and didn't laugh at my budget. He showed me a vacant house that smelled bad with ceilings that had collapsed from a water leak. It was missing appliances and had an uneven kitchen floor with a dip so deep you could drop a marble in the center of the room and have to chase it downhill till it bumped up against a baseboard. Nobody wanted this house.

I had the home inspected and was assured the house was structurally sound: "With a few repairs and some elbow grease, she would be a great home."

That Christmas Eve, I bought the house for a little less than 50 cents on the dollar and got it cleaned up. Then, I took one end and rented it to a law student, and later to a nurse. I got to play a small part in their advancement and success just by providing a comfortable home and affordable shelter for a time.

Using that rent money, I was able to pay off the house in less than 12 years.

Finding a home with a separate living unit, a finished bonus room, or a mother-in-law suite can open the door to rentals or hosting an Airbnb that can offer you a cushy second income.

That separate living unit could also provide a way to care for an aging or handicapped loved one without the expense of a rehab or assisted living facility. Check the covenants and restrictions for your neighborhood before purchasing.

Wendy Weaver

Single Mom in College Stashes More Cash

Let me introduce you to Wendy Weaver, a young single mom, recently divorced, in college earning her counseling degree. Even when child support wasn't enough, Wendy still dared to believe she could pursue her dream *and* make enough money to support her two little children.

Necessity is the mother of invention, and that held true for Wendy.

She searched for cheaper housing and found a large seven-room apartment that needed plumbing repairs and major clean-up just to be habitable.

Wendy made a deal with the landlord to have a friend fix the plumbing, and she would clean, polish, and paint the apartment in exchange for a 3-year lease at half the market rent. The landlord agreed, and Wendy rented two of the extra rooms to university students. That provided more than enough income to stay in school and finish her degree.

After obtaining her degree and license, and overcoming a few more setbacks, Wendy landed a great job as a professional counselor. She bought her own home in an area where she could raise chickens and have eggs to trade and sell on the side. Wendy knows how to make real estate pay *her* to enjoy living in her own home.

Amelia Allison

Be Frugal, Be Focused

Let me introduce you to Amelia Allison. Amelia left her parents' home right after high school and launched into an adventurous life traveling around the country. As one leg in her expeditions, Amelia got financial aid for a college in a place far from home. The young college student shared rent with fellow students and supported herself through a part-time job.

Amelia had planned ahead. She was frugal and focused. After graduating, she already intended to buy a home, but adventure still called. In order to travel and dive into life head-first, she needed a second income ... but how, without having to work a second job?

Inventive thinking inspired Amelia to purchase a house with four living units. She would live in one and rent the others.

First, rental income would more than cover the house note. Over time, rents would increase but her 30-year fixed rate would remain stable and low, increasing positive cash flow to fuel her excitement-seeking habits.

To accomplish her master plan, Amelia hired a knowledgeable realtor who knew the home market and the right professionals—the lender (me), a good home inspector, title company, insurance professional, and trustworthy handyman. I got her approved for a government, low fixed-rate, low down payment loan program.

Once the seller agreed to help with closing costs, Amelia and I went treasure hunting for down payment funds to get her into the property without disturbing her emergency fund.

I have to admit, hearing Amelia's plans made me yearn to step back in time for just a little while … to be in my twenties again. Amelia had her whole exciting life ahead of her. She knew what she wanted and how she was going to get there … and had the wherewithal to achieve it.

Adding Income to the Budget by Subdividing

Adele Edmond

Subdivide and Conquer

Adele Edmond was a divorced single mom of two middle-school daughters. She worked full time and wanted to give her daughters a good life. After the divorce, Adele kept their small house sitting off a highway outside city limits, where they'd lived for the last few years. Behind the house were ten acres that required care and maintenance.

Adele wanted a larger home in a district where her daughters' church friends attended school, but the houses there were above her financial ability. With little savings for a healthy down payment, the monthly mortgage would be too high.

Adele, however, wasn't taking no for an answer. After talking to some business and real estate savvy friends at church, she decided that instead of selling her current property, she would sub-divide the land and sell the lots individually. She partnered with a developer and a builder, and a trusted real estate friend.

Adele's venture is still underway, but I can tell you she is about set to make significantly more profit subdividing and selling the individual plots of land than she ever would have just selling the tiny house with the oversized backyard (and 10 acres of grass to mow).

From the proceeds thus far, Adele already has enough to make a sizeable down payment. This will secure a low monthly mortgage, and plenty of cash so she and her girls can live comfortably in the larger home in their preferred school district, with money left over to invest in their future.

Resources

https://www.daveramsey.com/budgeting/how-to-budget

CHAPTER 4

Conventional Mortgages

Housing is absolutely essential to human flourishing. Without stable shelter, it all falls apart.

Matthew Desmond

AFTER LISTENING INTENTLY to a customer's story, I get excited to find the very best loan product that will help them get from where they are to where they want to be with the least amount of expense. I evaluate credit, income, and money needed to close the transaction. It often comes down to a comparison between a government FHA loan program and a conventional loan. For clients with higher credit scores and a little extra money to put down, the conventional loan often wins.

The Conventional Loan

Advantages: For borrowers with high credit scores and a little extra money to put down, the conventional loan is structured so the borrower pays much less over time for private insurance.

Disadvantage: The conventional loan is not as forgiving on low credit scores. This loan program can sometimes be stricter on debt-to-income ratios.

Some down payment assistance programs will work with the conventional loan, but some programs may make it more difficult for the buyer to get the assistance when they are trying to use a conventional program.

Tip: When down payment is 10% or less, have the lender compare move-in costs and payment structure on the FHA loan and the conventional program. Assuming credit scores are excellent, the conventional loan usually requires the borrower to pay the least amount of mortgage insurance. Since mortgage insurance benefits the lender and not the borrower, the less private mortgage insurance the borrower has to pay, the more money he saves.

Example:
John and Jess Jamison were under contract to purchase their first home. This home had everything they wanted, including the pool in the back and a home office right inside the front door. Elation ran high as they imagined moving into this beautiful home and inviting their friends to enjoy it with them.

Stepping outside the euphoria and back into logical thinking mode, Jess sent a text to the lender asking to compare the FHA low-down-payment financing scenario to the conventional 5% down.

"We plan to stay in this house for a long time. We want to get rid of paying the mortgage insurance as soon as we can," Jess tapped out on the text.

The price of the house was $250,000. John and Jess could pay up to 10% down, but since the seller did not agree to pay their closing costs and prepaid taxes and insurance, they decided to pay down 5% or less, making the FHA scenario more attractive.

The FHA loan with a 3.5% down payment looked something like this:

Down payment:	$8,750
Closing costs:	$4,000
Prepaid taxes and insurance:	$5,000
	= $17,750

On the FHA loan program John and Jess would have to add 1.85% of the base loan amount to the final balance, as well as make *monthly* payments of .85% of the base loan amount for FHA mortgage insurance.

The base loan amount was $241,250. With the upfront FHA mortgage insurance, John and Jess would pay back a total loan amount of $245,241. Their starting fee would be about $171/month, which is .85% of the base loan amount divided over 12 months.

The conventional 5% down payment program looked something like this:

Down payment:	$12,500
Closing costs:	$4,000
Prepaid taxes and insurance	$5,000
	= $21,500

Unlike the FHA loan program, the conventional product did NOT add any upfront lender mortgage insurance to the loan, and the monthly insurance was only $58, which would disappear once the loan was paid down under 78% loan-to-value (LTV).

NOTE: There was an option on the conventional program for the borrower to pay one lump sum for private mortgage insurance under $3,000 and enjoy making no monthly private insurance payment at all, but they chose the monthly payment to pay down the loan to under 78% LTV early and get rid of the mortgage insurance payment.

After doing the math, John and Jess realized that the conventional loan was the best option for them. They would save a considerable amount of money over the time they planned to remain in the home.

Conventional mortgages are not insured or guaranteed by a government agency. On mortgages with a loan-to-value of over 80%, private mortgage insurance companies agree to pay the lender for a portion of the loss if the borrower defaults. Either the borrower or the lender pays for the private mortgage insurance, depending on pricing. The interest rate is higher on mortgages when the lender has to pay the private mortgage insurance.

Example:

Sale price/value (whichever is less):	$200,000
Loan amount:	$180,000
$180,000 divided by $200,000	= 90% LTV

Since the loan amount is greater than 80%, the lender will require the borrower to pay private mortgage insurance.

If the loan amount was $160,000, the LTV would be 80% or less and no private mortgage insurance would be needed.

There are two basic types of conventional mortgages.

Conforming loans do not exceed the amount annually set by the FHFA. These are eligible to be underwritten by the lender under the loan program guidelines and sold to Fannie Mae or Freddie Mac, the biggest mortgage buyers in the nation. Conforming conventional loans must meet the specific conventional loan program guidelines. The maximum loan limits differ based on county, and can be determined by checking websites for Fannie Mae and Freddie Mac.

Non-conforming loans are higher than the loan limits set by the FHFA and have different loan requirements than those set by Fannie Mae and Freddie Mac. A "Jumbo Loan" is an example of a non-conforming loan. Another example is a privately funded loan that does not meet the guidelines for Fannie Mae or Freddie Mac.

Maximum Loan-to-value on conforming loans depends on the borrower's credit score, number of units in the property, and how the borrower will use the property; for example, as a principal residence, a second home, or rental property. Also, the maximum loan-to-value can be affected by whether the mortgage will be for purchasing or refinancing the home.

Minimum Down Payments for Single-Family, Owner-Occupied

5% (only 3% for some special affordable products) for principal residence

10% for second homes or vacation homes

15% to 20% for investment property

20% to avoid paying private mortgage insurance

A single-family home on a refinance **with no cash out** can be up to 95% loan-to-value

Maximum Loan-to-Value for Single-Family Refinancing with Cash Out, Owner-Occupied

75% to 80% of the appraised value (some restrictions apply) for principal residence

75% of the appraised value for second homes and investment property

Maximum Debt-to-Income (DTI) Ratios

Mortgage underwriting software can sometimes approve borrowers for higher debt, so the borrower should determine their comfort level on a house payment. The maximum DTI ratio for a manually underwritten loan is 36% of gross qualified income. Underwriting can increase this ratio up to 45% when the loan meets certain criteria. The automated underwriting software often accepts an debt-to-income ratio of up to 50% of qualifying income.

Reserves include money available after the loan closing to use in case of emergencies. Required reserves are calculated according to the new house note. Some loan programs require two to six months of house payments in reserves after closing. Other financed real estate may also be factored into reserve requirements. The formulas to calculate may vary from one loan program to another. If the underwriting software does not require reserves, then no reserves would have to be verified.

Example:

At the time of this writing in the year 2020, Fannie Mae's conventional program has a graduated table in their guidelines for calculating reserve requirements.

If the borrower owns one to three financed real estate properties including the primary residence, the monthly amount of the subject property's house payment, including principal, interest, taxes and insurance, private mortgage insurance, and any homeowner association fees, is multiplied times two months. So, if the monthly payment including all the taxes and insurance, mortgage insurance, and association fees is $1,000/month, the reserve money needed comes to $1,000 × 2 = $2,000.

For the remaining financed real estate properties, add up the balances owed and multiply by 2%. If the total owed on the other two properties comes to $200,000, then multiply that by 2% for an additional $4,000 that would need to be verified in reserves on the day of closing. For all three properties, this borrower would need to show a total of $6,000 in reserves on the day of closing.

Reserve requirements are higher for borrowers who own eight or more financed properties.

Maximum financed properties allowed including the primary residence and second homes is six if the borrower is getting approved on a Freddie Mac program, or ten for Fannie Mae.

Interested Party Contributions are limited depending on loan-to-value. A seller or other interested party may pay for the buyer's closing costs, prepaid taxes and insurance, and buy-down points:

up to 3% of the sale price if the borrower is putting less than 10% down,

up to 6% of the sale price if the borrower is putting down 10% to 25%, up to 9% of the sale price if the borrower is putting down more than 25%.

If the borrower is buying an investment property, the interested parties cannot pay more than 2% of the sale price toward the borrower's costs. Also, on investment property loans, gift funds are not allowed.

Gifts are allowed (except on investment property) if properly documented from a family member or other significant relationship. Donors may not have any affiliation with the builder, developer, real estate agent, or other interested parties.

Cosigners are allowed.

Affordable Conventional Loan Programs

I fondly remember stories from first-time homebuyer clients who had been told they could never buy their own home because they needed too much money for the down payment, and a huge income. It was always a victory celebration at closing when they got to buy their home with zero or very little down using their own income to qualify. The realtor, closing attorney, and I clapped and cheered as our clients held the keys to their new homes.

Affordable programs are available to borrowers with limited funds for down payment and whose credit scores are lower than the traditional borrower. To qualify for the affordable programs, borrowers must not exceed the household income limit for their area.

Three common conventional affordable programs are:

1. Fannie Mae's HomeReady program
2. Freddie Mac's Home Possible program
3. Community 97 program

These programs are similar to the regular conventional programs but are more lenient on lower credit scores. They require less down payment and sometimes community second mortgages can be used with them to reduce the amount of funds needed at closing.

The cost of private mortgage insurance is less on the affordable loan programs.

The borrower must complete an eight-hour Homebuyers Education Course from a HUD-approved homebuyer education school.

There are more down payment assistance programs available for the affordable conventional programs than for the regular conventional mortgage product.

(Check links to the resources listed below and check the latest guidelines.)

Rochelle Murdoch

A Dream Come True

Rochelle Murdoch heaved the brown moving box labeled "CDs & DVDs" off the sofa, plunking it down on the nearby end table. She collapsed into the one open spot on the sofa between boxes, kicking her legs up on the coffee table to rest.

At 40 years old, Rochelle felt the satisfying sense of accomplishment on owning her first house. Her family and friends would return the next day to continue the celebration. They would help her unpack, hang curtains and transform the house into her own sanctuary—her very own home.

Rochelle had always thought owning a house required lots of money down and a high mortgage payment. A real estate agent she met at church showed her that with an affordable loan and low-interest rate she could get into a house for a minimum of $500 with payments lower than her rent—not to mention the tax write-off on the mortgage interest.

Rochelle could only ask, "Why didn't I do this sooner?"

Key Puzzle Piece: Rochelle had low credit scores and only $500 to put down. She needed to keep her payment as low as possible.

Mortgage Solution: The Affordable Lending Program offered Rochelle flexible credit guidelines and only a minimum contribution from her own funds. The seller was allowed to pay her closing cost and prepaid taxes and insurance. The monthly private mortgage insurance was much less expensive compared to the standard conventional loan programs, keeping Rochelle's payments much lower than if she had tried to use a traditional conventional mortgage. The product allowed her to get some down payment assistance in the form of a community second mortgage.

Affordable loan programs are designed for borrowers who may not have traditional credit lines/credit scores. It can approve borrowers who do not have a two-year credit history on most credit sources. It allows for more types of income to be considered, such as boarder income. The affordable loan products sometimes allow a first and second mortgage combination up to 105% combined loan-to-value.

Max Loan Amount: Determined by a customer's qualified income, which must fall within a stated percentage of the Area Median Income, which varies yearly.

Cosigner: Allowed, but only under certain conditions.

Documentation: Fully documented. The borrower is permitted to use qualified secondary income, such as boarder income.

Minimum Down Payment: 3%

For one unit, the borrower's closing costs, prepaids, or down payment may come from the following sources:

- Gift
- Unsecured loan or grant from a government agency, borrower's employer, or non-profit organization.
- Secured borrower funds such as life insurance policy, 401(k), etc.
- Community second mortgage or non-community second.

Cash-on-hand is acceptable with some restrictions.

Mortgage Insurance: Required mortgage insurance is significantly less than on traditional high loan-to-value loans for one-unit properties. Mortgage insurance can be paid monthly or in one lump sum added to the loan, up to a maximum of 97% loan-to-value. Pricing and availability of private mortgage insurance varies according to loan-to-value and credit scores.

Occupancy: Primary Residence.

Prepayment Penalty: None.

Resources

https://singlefamily.fanniemae.com/originating-underwriting/loan-limits (Conventional Loan Limits)

https://entp.hud.gov/idapp/html/hicostlook.cfm (FHA loan limits)

https://singlefamily.fanniemae.com/originating-underwriting/ mortgage-products/homeready-mortgage (Latest information on Fannie Mae HomeReady Affordable Program)

http://www.freddiemac.com/homepossible/index.html (Latest information on Freddie Mac Home Possible Affordable Program)

https://singlefamily.fanniemae.com/originating-underwriting/mortgage-products/97-loan-value-options (Conventional 97 Mortgage Program)

CHAPTER 5

The FHA Loan Program

You will never leave where you are until you decide where you would rather be.

Anonymous

THE GOVERNMENT FHA (Federal Housing Administration) loan program has been a godsend to so many with lower credit scores, lighter savings, and higher debt. It is also more forgiving towards lower down payments. I have seen the FHA loan help one family after another glide into a new home, securing the keys not only to a new home but to a better life.

FHA Low Down Payment and Mortgage Insurance

The FHA mortgage program operates under HUD (Housing and Urban Development), offering government-insured loans. It allows buyers to put down as little as 3.5% of the sale price or appraised value, whichever is less.

On FHA loans with a loan-to-value of 90% or more, FHA charges a monthly mortgage insurance fee of .85% of the base loan amount, which is the amount before upfront mortgage insurance of 1.75% is added to the balance. This .85% FHA monthly fee remains for the life of the loan.

When the FHA loan is less than 90% loan-to-value or for a 15-year term or less, the monthly mortgage insurance rate is less.

Example:

Sale price: $100,000

Down payment: 3.5% × $100,000 = $3,500

Base loan amount: $100,000 - $3,500 = $96,500

$96,500 × .85% = ~$820/12 months = $68.35/month

To insure lenders in the case of buyer default, FHA charges an upfront fee by adding 1.75% of the base loan amount onto the loan balance.

Example:

Sale price: $100,000

Down payment: $3,500

Base loan amount: $96,500

FHA adds the 1.75% upfront mortgage insurance to the top of the base loan:

$96,500 × 1.0175 = $98,188, representing the $1,688 upfront funding fee added to the base loan.

Check the HUD website and search for "Mortgage Insurance" to get the most up-to-date tables and charts calculating the upfront and monthly mortgage insurance from FHA.

Tom and Bria Anderson

The Perfect House with the Perfect Financing

Tom and Bria Anderson were excited about their future even though the young couple still had a year left till graduation from pharmacy school. They had found the perfect house in one of their favorite neighborhoods.

The problem? The Andersons were living on student loan stipends, a type of income that cannot be used for loan qualification on most standard loan programs. The beautiful $160,000 house was beginning to look unobtainable ... until their loan officer started putting the puzzle pieces together.

Key Puzzle Piece #1: Bria's parents agreed to co-sign on the loan. Her parents had good credit, a conservative amount of debt, and enough income to qualify for the Andersons' note.

Mortgage Solution: Some conventional loans require the occupying borrowers to have enough income to qualify at a minimum debt-to-income ratio. However, the FHA 30-year fixed rate loan allows the family-related co-signer to fully qualify for the loan even if the occupying borrowers have no qualified income.

The FHA loan also required only a 3.5% down payment and allowed the sellers to pay up to 6% of the sale price toward closing costs, prepaid property taxes, and homeowners insurance.

The Andersons liked the fixed rate on the FHA loan because they planned to live in the house for over five years and did not want the payment to increase.

The adjustable-rate FHA loan adjusts once annually. There are annual and lifetime safety caps limiting how much the interest rate can move.

The FHA 3-1 ARM and 5-1 ARM stay fixed for the first three and five years, respectively. After the fixed term, rates adjust annually with annual and lifetime safety caps.

FHA also offers a 7-1 ARM and 10-1 ARM. All of these loan types have their own advantages.

FHA Fixed Rate

Max Loan Amount: Announced annually. Entp.hud.gov site tells you the maximum base loan amount for your county and state for a single unit home. There is usually a higher maximum allowed loan amount for a two-unit property and an even higher amount for multi-unit properties.

Cosigner: Allowed if they have a principal residence in the U.S. To use maximum financing, the non-occupant co-borrower must not be associated with the transaction, and qualify as a "relative" either by blood or close family-like relationship according to FHA standards. Otherwise, the maximum loan-to-value is 75%.

Documentation: Fully documented.

Minimum Down Payment: Must be at least 3.5% of either the sale price or appraisal, whichever is less (or can be as low as zero with specific down payment assistance programs).

Mortgage Insurance: Upfront and monthly on FHA loans.

Occupancy: Primary residence—a borrower owning a principal residence with an FHA mortgage may not purchase another principal residence with an FHA loan except under special circumstances.

Second Home: With restrictions.

Investment Property: With restrictions.

Prepayment Penalty: None.

Property Types: 1-4 units.

Ratios: House payment to gross income determines the housing ratio. On manually underwritten loans, the maximum housing ratio is 31% and the total debt including new house note cannot exceed 43% of gross income. (These are suggested ratios. **With other compensating factors much higher ratios are sometimes allowed through automatic underwriting programs.**)

Subordinate Financing: Allowed if it is from a governmental or HUD-approved non-profit agency or from a family member (other exceptions and restrictions apply).

Seller Contributions: Up to 6% of the sale price or appraised value, whichever is less.

Source of Funds: Gifts allowed with documentation and some restrictions.

Assumable: The FHA loan is an assumable loan, but the assuming party is required to qualify with the current lender servicing the loan. If the borrower's FHA mortgage has a 3% fixed rate and the market has now moved to 6%, the borrower could sell the home and advertise that she has an FHA loan than can be assumed at the 3% rate as long as the new homebuyer qualifies with the borrower's lender who is actively servicing the loan at the time of the assumption.

Term: 30 years and 15 years on fixed-rate FHA loans.

Resources

www.hud.gov

CHAPTER 6

The Veteran Home Loan Program

The true soldier fights, not because he hates what is in front of him, but because he loves what is behind him.

G.K. Chesterton

THE VETERAN LOAN program has given our deserving military veterans hope for a good future after a life committed to serving our country. Not only does the VA loan allow them to own a home with zero or little money down, but owning the home offers safety, security, and a base to build wealth.

Veteran Loan Advantages

The VA assists veterans in financing their home with zero or little down at closing. VA sets their own rules for loan qualification, but does not lend the money. Instead, they guarantee a portion of the loan. Should the borrower default, the VA promises to pay the lender a percentage of their mortgage.

The "zero down" opportunity is one of the biggest advantages of the VA loan program. Another is the elimination of monthly mortgage insurance. There is, however, an upfront funding fee, which can vary depending on the borrower's status with VA. Many times, the upfront VA funding fee is waived if the veteran is considered by VA to be disabled. Check **www. VA.gov** to determine the amount of the upfront VA funding fee.

Eligibility Guidelines

The veteran needs to apply for the VA "Certificate of Eligibility" (COE) to determine eligibility and exactly how much of his eligibility is available to use. The lender will lend four times the amount of available eligibility. If that is still not enough to cover the mortgage on the house in question, then consult with your lender. Most will go much higher than eligibility.

VA Home Loan Eligibility

To be eligible, a veteran must meet ONE or more of these requirements:
- **90 consecutive days of active service during wartime**, or
- **181 days of active service during peacetime**, or
- **6 years of service in the National Guard or Reserves**, or
- You are the **spouse of a service member who has died** in the line of duty or as a result of a service-related disability.

Wayne Tozer

Back from Duty and Ready to Make a House a Home

It had been a long overseas tour. Wayne Tozer's eyes anxiously combed over the sea of grandmas and grandpas, mothers and fathers, and children. Some waved small American flags; others had posters with "Welcome Home Our Heroes" written on them.

Wayne's heart skipped a beat. Seeing his wife holding their three-year-old son took his breath away. Instantly, the soldier was moving through the jostling crowd to reunite with his family. They didn't see him coming. He was greeted with surprise and unbridled joy when at last they met again.

Quickly upon his return, Wayne committed to a few short and long-term priorities:
- spend time with his family.
- settle into his new civilian job.
- purchase a home for his family to build equity and give them room to grow.

Wayne's credit was decent and his income enough to manage the house note—but he lacked the cash for the down payment and closing costs.

Immediately, we set about putting the pieces together.

Key Puzzle Pieces:
- (1) Wayne's veteran status and time in the military made him eligible for the zero down VA loan.
- (2) The sellers were willing to pay closing costs and prepaid property taxes and insurance.

Mortgage Solution: The VA Loan allows the eligible veteran to get a 100% loan. If the seller agrees to pay all of the closing costs and prepaid taxes and insurance, the veteran pays zero down to move in.

The VA programs offer fixed rate and adjustable-rate terms. Since the Tozer family planned on staying in the house for over five years, they chose the fixed rate. If they were not planning to stay more than three years, the adjustable-rate program with a fixed rate for the first three years might have been a good choice.

VA Fixed Rate

Max Loan Amount: Check out the VA website in the resources below to determine VA loan amounts permitted in your county and state. As of the writing of this book, your VA home loan limit is based on the county limit wherever the property is located. In case of default, the VA agrees to pay the lender up to 25% of the county loan limit.

Borrower Eligibility: The borrower must have served in the regular military a minimum of two years or the full term (at least 90 days in wartime and 181 days in peacetime).

Cosigner: Not applicable. The co-borrower can be married to the veteran or have his/her own VA eligibility. Must occupy the property.

Documentation: Fully documented.

Minimum Down Payment: Zero.

VA Funding Fee: The VA funding fee can be paid in cash at closing or it can be rolled into the loan, provided the loan does not exceed the maximum allowed. The seller, lender, or veteran can pay the funding fee. The amount of the funding fee varies according to the down payment amount, type of military service, and term of the loan. For a veteran from the regular military using his entitlement for the first time with zero down, the rate would be 2.3% of the loan amount. There is no monthly VA funding fee (some exceptions).

Check the veteran website in the resources and search for "Funding Fee Chart."

Occupancy: Primary Residence.

Prepayment Penalty: None.

Property Types: 1-4 units.

Ratios: 41% is the suggested maximum DTI ratio. The VA loan program also considers other factors such as the estimated maintenance cost of the house, square footage, etc.

Income: Veteran mortgages use two different calculations to determine the veteran's capacity to maintain the mortgage payment.

The first method divides qualified gross income by the total monthly debt payments, which include association fees plus the full house payment with taxes and insurance.

Example:

Gross income: $4,500/month

Proposed new house note: $1,500/month ($1,000 P&I plus $500 for property taxes and insurance)

Other debt: Car note of $400/month + $35/month minimum revolving credit payment = $435

House payment of $1,500 + $435 in "other" debt = $1,935/month

Debt-to-income ratio = total debt/income = $1,935/$4,500 = 43%

The second method calculates residual income. The residual income formula considers the number of household members, taxable income, state taxes, social security, Medicare deductions, and the gross living area. If the DTI is higher than 41% on the first calculation, then the residual income must exceed the VA guideline by 20% and meet certain compensating factors.

Subordinate Financing: Allowed under certain conditions.

Seller Contributions: Up to 4% of the sale price or appraised value, whichever is less.

Source of Funds: Gifts are allowed with documentation and some restrictions.

Term: Fixed 30-year and 15-year terms.

Adjustable-Rate: 30-year term (check availability because ARM products are not always available).

Assumable: With some restrictions; borrower must qualify with the lender servicing the mortgage at the time of the assumption.

Resources

www.va.gov (for maximum loan limits by state and county. Charts defining varying amounts of VA funding fees charged, availability of various types of VA loan programs)

CHAPTER 7

USDA Rural Housing Program

A bright future for the nation depends on the health and prosperity of rural America.

Kirsten Gillibrand

THE USDA RURAL Housing loan has been the perfect solution for those who want a 100% loan and prefer living away from the crush of the big city. With household income within the USDA limit for the county, and the property in an eligible area, the USDA loan has made the difference between some of my clients owning a home or continuing to rent. It is a pleasure to see their smiling faces at the closing table as these clients sign on the dotted line for the USDA Rural Housing loan program.

The Government USDA Rural Housing Loan

The purpose of the USDA Loan is to provide affordable homeownership financing to promote prosperity in rural communities, improving the quality of rural life.

The USDA loan program guarantees the lender 90% of the loan amount if the borrower defaults, lowering lenders' risk to 10% of the loan and offering the borrower the chance for a 100% loan with zero down.

There are two basic types of Rural Housing lending programs.

The first is the Single-Family Housing Direct Home Loan (Direct Loan), where borrowers go directly to their local USDA office to obtain the loan.

The other is the Single-Family Housing Guaranteed Loan Program (SFHGLP or Guaranteed Loan Program). The Guaranteed Loan Program is offered by lenders approved through the USDA Rural Housing Agency.

What Does the USDA Rural Housing Loan Do for Borrowers?

Eligible applicants using the 502 Guaranteed Loan Program get a 100% loan for purchasing an adequate, modest, decent, safe, and sanitary dwelling as their primary residence in eligible rural areas. Borrowers who are approved on the USDA Rural Housing loan may purchase, build, rehabilitate, improve, or relocate a dwelling in an eligible rural area with 100% financing.

The Single-Family Housing Repair Loans and Grants Program provides grants and funds for elderly or disabled low-income homeowners to make necessary repairs and modifications to their home, or to make it more energy-efficient.

- Single-Family Housing Direct Home Loans
- Single-Family Housing Home Loan Guarantees
- Mutual Self-Help Housing Technical Assistance Grants
- Rural Housing Site Loans
- Single-Family Housing Repair Loans & Grants | Rural Development (usda.gov)

How to Qualify for a USDA Rural Housing Loan

Applicants must meet household income eligibility, not to exceed 115% of the median household income for their state and county. (See link in the resources at the end of this chapter to check your eligibility.)

The property must be located in an eligible, less populated area as determined by USDA Rural Housing mapping. (See link in the resources to discover property eligibility.)

The applicant must be a U.S. Citizen, U.S. non-citizen national, or Qualified Alien.

There are two Rural Housing program fees. At the time of this writing, the first is the upfront mortgage insurance of around 1%.

Example:

Sale price: $200,000

Base loan amount: $200,000

1% USDA Upfront mortgage fee = 1% × $200,000 = ... $2,000

Total fee: $200,000 + $2,000 = ... $202,000

The second is the monthly insurance covering the lender in case of default, which is currently around .35% of the unpaid balance.

Base loan amount: $200,000

Monthly Insurance: $200,000 × .0035 = $700/12 = $58.33/month until the loan is paid down to 80% loan-to-value.

Income eligibility is determined after calculating **all household income** including household members not needed to qualify for the loan, such as a non-borrowing spouse, adult family member(s) such as elderly parents, and children over 18 not currently in school.

USDA has stricter guidelines for DTI and housing ratios. A borrower might get approved with a little higher-than-normal DTI or housing debt ratio, but the borrower would need to document compensating factors.

Qualifying ratio for the proposed house payment is 29% for Principal Interest Taxes and Insurance (PITI) and any association fees. Total DTI ratio is 41% of qualified gross income.

Example:

House payment: $1,000

PITI (including USDA monthly fees plus taxes and insurance)

Other monthly debt: $600

Total monthly debt: $1,000 + $600 = ... $1,600

Qualified income: $4,000

Housing ratio: $1,000/$4,000 (25%)

Debt-to-income ratio: $1,600/ $4,000 (40%)

Bo Binkins

Bo's Grand Escape

Bo Binkins never liked city life. He grew up in the city because his father was a successful mechanic for a trucking company, but whenever he and his family went camping, hunting, and fishing in the land their family owned his soul felt free. The smell of the flowers, the feel of the breeze in his hair, the sounds of tweeting birds and splashing fish on the end of his line made him come alive.

As a kid, he visualized himself hauling his fishing boat behind a truck and parking next to his farmhouse in the country. Year after year, Bo worked, just like his dad, as a mechanic in a big shop downtown. When he got married, his wife and children became the focus of his time and almost *all* of his money. Getting to go fishing with his dad and friends now and again kept his soul happy, but he yearned to live every day in the wide-open country.

Several times, Bo tried to get approved for a house in the country but kept getting turned down. Either the house was too beat up or his credit scores were too low. Bo felt hopeless, but his wife and friends encouraged him not to give up.

One day, while fishing with his brother, they dreamed together out loud. Seeing his hunger for the dream, Bo's brother suggested that he visit a loan officer to get help with his credit and find a loan that did not require a lot of money down.

He did just that ... and together we got it done.

The day Bo Binkins got preapproved for the 100% USDA Rural Housing loan was an ecstatic one, surpassed only by the day he closed on that little farmhouse in the country, its covered shed ready and awaiting his future boat. Bo could finally breathe the country air and found his life suddenly full of possibilities.

The 100% USDA Rural Housing Loan worked best for Bo because he had almost no down payment money. The sellers of the little farmhouse agreed to pay Bo's closing costs and prepaid taxes and insurance, so Bo got to buy his home with zero down.

With the USDA Rural Housing Program, he achieved affordable monthly payments thanks to a fixed rate that came in lower than the rates offered on conventional loan programs. The monthly fee was also less than those on other programs, and the USDA was more forgiving of his credit scores. Thanks to these incredible benefits from the Rural Housing program, Bo Binkins brought his life dream to reality.

Resources

https://eligibility.sc.egov.usda.gov/eligibility/incomeEligibilityAction. do?pageAction=state (USDA site to determine income eligibility)

https://eligibility.sc.egov.usda.gov/eligibility/welcomeAction.do?pageAction=sfp (USDA property eligibility)

Single-Family Housing Direct Home Loans | Rural Development (usda.gov)

Single-Family Housing Guaranteed Loan Program | Rural Development (usda. gov)

Mutual Self-Help Housing Technical Assistance Grants | Rural Development (usda.gov)

Rural Housing Site Loans | Rural Development (usda.gov)

Single Family Housing Repair Loans & Grants | Rural Development (usda.gov)

CHAPTER 8

State and Municipal Bond Assistance Programs

Buying a home is a big step up into another echelon of society, of respect, and of, well, responsibility ... that is 100 percent worth it.

www.HomeStratosphere.com

THE STATE AND Municipal Bond Assistance programs always reminded me of a generous and supportive uncle or aunt or family friend. Some of these programs are grants but some, like your uncle and aunt, expect to be repaid at some point.

State Bond Programs and Down Payment Assistance

Many states and local jurisdictions offer special loans or grants to encourage homeownership. The state or municipality may provide the funding for a mortgage, or a second mortgage, down payment assistance, or a grant at favorable rates under certain restrictions. Check with your lender or realtor to discover the programs available in your area. Check the resource links below.

According to the National Association of Realtors, at one time, 90% to 95% of people surveyed who said they needed down payment assistance were not aware of the many programs to assist them. There are about 2,000 down payment assistance programs available to first-time homebuyers across the United States.

If you want to know more, do an internet search for "Down Payment Assistance" with the name of your city and state … and you should hit the jackpot. You may even find special programs for groups such as teachers, police, firefighters, military, and other first-responders.

Four Basic Types of Down Payment Assistance Programs

1. **Soft second mortgages**—These second mortgages are forgiven over a set number of years. Some do not have to be repaid at all if the borrower continues to live in the home as a primary residence for the agreed-upon time.

2. **Second mortgages that are deferred**—These second mortgages do not require monthly payments. However, the loan would have to be paid off when the homeowner sells, moves, or refinances.

3. **First or second mortgages that have to be paid down**—Monthly payments begin right away and continue until the loan is paid off completely.

4. **Grants**—These are gifts that do not have to be repaid. Usually, the program has restrictions that the borrower must meet to qualify for the grant.

Ask an experienced, reputable realtor in your area what programs they recommend. Good realtors usually know which programs are good and which might be less advantageous. You can also check with Rob Chrane at **Down Payment Resource**, supported by Housing Finance Agencies across the country. From there, you can search for assistance programs in your city and state. (See link in the resources at the end of this chapter.)

How to Qualify for Down Payment Assistance

1. **First-time Homebuyer**—First-time Homebuyer status is sometimes required on state and municipal bond programs. A first-time homebuyer would be defined as someone who has not owned real estate in the last three years. There are exceptions to this rule for properties in certain census tracts that allow the borrower to waive

the first-time homebuyer status. Check with your local lender for more information.

2. **Household Income Limits**—Household income limits are usually restricted to 100% or 80% of the average median income for the state and county where the property is located. Household income is usually used by the bond program underwriters to determine eligibility. That means that if you are the only person on the loan and title but you are married, the bond program requires the spouse's income to be factored towards total household income. Check with your local lender for more information.

3. **Qualification for Two Different Loan Programs**—Lenders calculate your income based on any underlying loan program such as FHA, VA, or Conventional. These qualify only the borrower's and not necessarily household income, but the borrower's income and DTI must meet the first-lien lender's conditions.

The underwriters for the bond program review the loan package to make sure that the property and you, the borrower, meet their guidelines, which include verifying all income for anyone over 18 in the household. The guidelines for the first-lien or second-lien assistance programs tend to be stricter than the underwriting FHA, Conventional, VA, or USDA programs.

4. **Homebuyer Education Class**—A Homebuying Class approved by HUD is required for state and municipal bond and assistance programs. Contact your lender or the agency offering the assistance for costs, sign up instructions, and how to complete your class long before closing.

5. **Primary Residence Requirement**—Most of the state bond and municipal loan programs require the homebuyer to remain in the home as their primary residence for a certain number of years. If the homeowner leaves sooner than promised, the funds may have to be repaid immediately. Some programs forgive the second lien after a certain number of years. Check with your lender for details.

6. **Recapture Tax**—Some bond and down payment assistance programs contain clauses requiring the home buyer to pay a recapture tax if they sell the home ahead of contract. The recapture tax is calculated based on the comparison between the original sale price and the current higher sale price, among other factors.

7. **Maximum Sale Price**—"Acquisition Cost Limits" put a lid on the sale price of the home you can purchase using the assistance program.

8. **Income Property Prohibition**—Bond programs usually limit to single-family primary residences since their purpose is to provide a home and not an income property. Sometimes, these programs will prohibit not only renting the unit, but also using the home as a home office.

9. **Eligible Geographic Areas**—Some of these special programs require that the subject property is in a certain geographic location. For instance, the Tennessee Housing Development Program limits to Tennessee properties only.

Loan Types Typically Underlying Bond and Municipal Programs
Conventional Loan Programs
FHA Loan Programs
VA Loan Programs
Rural Development Loan Programs

Alia Abbey

Trauma to Triumph
When you know some of a client's personal story, it helps you appreciate even more their journey to finally achieving homeownership. This was certainly the case with Alia Abbey, a single woman who

sounded over the phone like she really wanted to buy her home, but kept trying to convince me why it would never happen.

When I talked to her the first time she said, "Look, I am calling you because I found a house that would be perfect for me. My realtor told me to call you to get preapproved, but I don't believe I can really buy a house. Every time I have tried in the past, some catastrophe hits my life and the deal falls through. So ... I gave up a long time ago."

Alia had okay credit and a good steady income, just not the money for down payment, and she had no idea about the down payment assistance programs available to her. We looked at one such program to project her monthly payment and calculate the tiny sum she would need at closing. For the first time, Alia let herself get excited.

Once approved, Alia's program would provide her with over $10,000 in the form of a second mortgage to apply toward her down payment and closing costs. After living in the home 15 years, the second mortgage would be considered satisfied even though she had never made a payment on it.

The first-lien was an FHA mortgage requiring only a 3.5% down payment. This FHA loan was funded by a state bond program with a lower-than-market mortgage interest rate. By using this program along with the second mortgage down payment assistance, Alia could keep her emergency funds in place and easily afford the monthly mortgage note.

As we got closer to closing, Alia started getting cold feet! Suddenly, she was once again ready to sabotage her chance of owning a home.

I started asking questions.

She shared about a traumatic childhood experience when her family's home was destroyed by a catastrophic event.

BINGO!

With the encouragement of Alia's realtor, her friends at work, and of course the mortgage team, this lady went to her closing and laughed, then cried (for joy), and then laughed again. With the help of a down payment assistance program and some great real estate professionals, buying her own home was not just about owning a house, it was a breakthrough and a turning point for Alia Abbey.

Resources

http://downpaymentresource.com/about/leadership/ You can also check with Rob Chrane at Down Payment Resource, supported by Housing Finance Agencies across the country, for assistance programs in YOUR city and state.

www.thda.org Tennessee Housing Development Agency

https://www.memphistn.gov/government/housing-and-community-development/down-payment-assistance-program/ City of Memphis (TN) Down Payment Assistance

https://www.develop901.com/hosing/homeOwnership Shelby County (TN) Down Payment Assistance

CHAPTER 9

The Adjustable-Rate Mortgage

Be clear about your goal but be flexible about the process of achieving it.

Brian Tracy

THERE ARE MANY hall-of-fame stories I could tell when it comes to the adjustable-rate mortgage programs. The adjustable-rate is like a strong, spicy ingredient you use in a recipe. It is dynamic and delightful in certain foods ... and absolutely awful in others.

When considering an adjustable-rate mortgage, you need to be clear on your goal, know what you are trying to accomplish, and understand how long it will take.

Historically and under most market conditions the adjustable-rate mortgage (ARM) has enabled borrowers to enjoy a lower rate of interest with a lower payment than on fixed rate programs, at least in the beginning. In this arrangement, both borrower and lender share the risk of economic change and rate fluctuations over time. The fixed-rate mortgage program is the most popular and stable, but under some circumstances, the ARM program offers attractive options and advantages.

Components of the ARM

Index. The index is the "benchmark" starting point lenders use to compute adjustable-rate mortgage interest over a set time period. Common indexes are treasury bills or securities, 11th District Cost of Funds, Federal Home Loan Bank Rate, and more.

Margin. At the end of the initial loan period, a margin of usually two to three percent is added to the index. Whereas the overall rate may change and fluctuate, the margin will always remain the same for the life of the loan.

Initial Rate. Some lenders call this the "teaser rate." It is usually about a full point to half a point less than the fixed mortgage rate, compelling some borrowers to use the product.

Adjustment Period. Each ARM program sets up adjustment periods.

Some programs are set for a rate change once per year. Others stay fixed for the first three years before converting to a yearly adjustable. Still, other hybrid ARM programs are fixed for the first three, five, seven, or ten years before converting to a yearly adjustable. At each adjustment, the payment is recalculated based on the new rate and unpaid balance.

Caps. Safety caps are put in place on ARM programs to prevent the interest rate from spiking suddenly in a run-away interest market. The two most common caps are the annual and the lifetime caps. The annual cap limits the yearly rate change to a 1%-2% increase or decrease. The lifetime cap limits the maximum that the interest rate can move over the life the of the loan. The cap is usually 5% or 6% over the start rate. For example, if the start rate is 4% and the cap rate is 6%, then the maximum interest could go as high as 10%.

Assumability. Most ARM programs allow for another party to assume and take over the payments on the mortgage as long as they qualify with the lender holding the note. This is an added protection for the original borrower, just in case the rate and payments ratchet too high for them to effectively handle with their finances.

Conversion. Check the terms of the ARM program you are considering. Some have options to convert to a fixed-rate at certain points during the term of the loan. There may be an extra cost to activate the conversion clause.

Disadvantages of Using the ARM

1. The increase in rate and payments may cause hardship to the borrower.

2. If the market conditions over the term of the ARM cause the rates to go up at every adjustment, this could cause the borrower to pay a lot more interest over time than if they had used the fixed-rate program instead.

3. The borrower shares the risk of economic market changes with the lender.

Advantages of Using the ARM

1. There is more borrowing power if the ARM rate is lower than the fixed-rate program. If the rate is lower and the payment is lower, you might even qualify for a higher loan amount. Keep in mind that on some ARM programs lenders qualify you at the highest possible rate at the first adjustment.

2. The flexibility of the ARM program can help the borrower who will be able to pay 50% or more of the owed balance on the loan before the first adjustment. This is a big advantage because when the first rate adjustment occurs, the new payment is calculated *only on the unpaid balance.*

The Dodds

The Dodds came to me with a contract to buy their dream home but shared with me that they planned to retire in a couple of years. To get the mortgage payment low enough for them to afford after retirement, they needed a larger down payment than they had means to pay.

However, they were expecting a $100,000 inheritance within the next 12 months that would enable them to pay down over 50% of their current mortgage.

We considered asking the lender to recast their payment after paying down 50% of the loan. In this scenario, the Dodds' payment would be re-amortized to a lower monthly note based on the remaining mortgage balance after paying down the $100,000 lump sum.

In the end, they chose to take an ARM with safety caps. After looking at the worst-case scenario, they would benefit even in a market where rates increased because the payment on each yearly adjustment was figured only on the unpaid balance. Thankfully, they didn't even come near to the worst-case scenario as rates remained low during at least the first ten years of the life of their loan.

Here is the worst-case scenario based on mortgage rates at the time they were exploring options:

Sale price: $200,000
Down payment: $20,000
Loan amount: $180,000

Comparing the 1-year, Adjustable-Rate Mortgage

The initial rate on the 1-year adjustable during the year of this example was about 4% compared to the market 30-year fixed-rate at 6.5% during this same period. Annual safety caps prevent the rate from going up or down more than 2% at each annual change. The 6% lifetime safety cap prevents the mortgage rate from going up over the life of the loan more than 6% above the initial starting interest rate.

P&I payment at market 6.5% fixed mortgage rate = $1,137 per month.

P&I payment at the market level in the first year of the adjustable rate with 2% annual safety cap and 6% lifetime safety cap = $859/per month.

If the Dodds applied their $100,000 inheritance as a lump sum prepayment during the first twelve months of their home purchase, the monthly mortgage payment the following year would change substantially.

Second Year: Before making their prepayment, the second year rate moved up to its maximum 2% increase bringing the rate from 4% to 6%. At this point, the loan balance was $177,000. When the Dodds made the $100,000 prepayment, the balance dropped to $76,830.

With the loan amount paid down to approximately $76,830 at the 2nd year rate of 6% for the approximate 29 years/348 months left on the mortgage, the P&I came to $466/month.

Third Year: Balance paid down to approximately $75,755, If market rates are at worst case, mortgage rate for year three would move up the maximum annual two percentage points to 8% for a P&I payment of $566.16 per month. As you can see, that is still less than the initial P&I payment.

Fourth Year: Balance paid down to $75,014. If market rates are at worst case, mortgage rate for fourth year would move the maximum annual two percentage points to 10%, creating a P&I payment of $671.104 per month … still less than the initial payment.

Since the maximum lifetime cap on the Dodds' loan was six interest rate points above the initial starting rate of 4%, the rate could never go any higher than 10%. Since the mortgage balance would continue to decrease, the P&I would also continue to decrease. *See charts at the end of this chapter for a more detailed breakdown of possible scenarios.*

If the Dodds knew they would not receive the large lump sum to put down until after five to seven years, we would have explored future payments using the hybrid adjustable-rate programs that kept the initial rate fixed for the first five to seven years. Once the fixed-rate period ended on these hybrid programs, the remaining P&I monthly payments would be amortized by the mortgage company for the remaining years of the mortgage at the maximum rate allowed after calculating the margin, and the annual and lifetime safety caps.

Compare with the Possibility of Recasting

The Dodds considered that the lender might allow them to recast their mortgage payment once the $100,000 lump sum was paid. At that point, the lender could calculate a lower monthly payment for them by amortizing only the remaining balance of the loan at the same rate of 6.5% over the remaining 29 years of the loan. That would make the P&I payment $491.10 per month.

Whereas a refinance pays off the old loan and begins a brand new one, usually incurring additional closing costs, in a recast the lender keeps the same loan with the option to recalculate your payment on the unpaid balance, also keeping the same loan rate over the remaining term of the loan. The borrower must pay down at least twenty percent on the principal balance for recast to be an option.

Check with your lender to compare rates on the adjustable and fixed rate mortgage programs. Due to inverted market conditions or investor appetites, adjustable rates can sometimes be higher than the fixed rates.

CHOOSING THE BEST MORTGAGE

Basic Loan Information	
Loan Amount	$76,830.00
Initial Interest Rate on Loan	6.00%
Loan Term (in months) approximately 29 years left after prepaymt	**348 months**
Initial Payment Amount	$466.37
Rate Adjustments & Minimum/Maximum Rates	
Rate Index Base Value	4.00%
Margin	2.00%
Number of Months to 1st Adjustment	12 months
Maximum Rate Change on 1st Adjustment	2.00%
Duration Between Subsequent Rate Adjustments	12 months
Subsequent Rate Adjustments	6.00%
Maximum Interest Rate over Life of Mortgage	10.00%
Minimum Interest Rate over Life of Mortgage	4.00%
Assumptions about Future Interest Rates	
Worst Case: the interest rate index jumps to 100% in month 2	
Upward Movement Index Rate Starts Rising in Year:	2
Upward Movement Index Rate Rises for:	10 years
Upward Movement Index Rate Rises By:	2.00% per year

The Adjustable-Rate Mortgage

Month	Worst Case			Up Trend		
	ARM Rate	Payment	Balance	ARM Rate	Payment	Balance
1	6.000%	466.37	76,747.78	6.000%	466.37	76,747.78
2	6.000%	466.37	76,665.15	6.000%	466.37	76,665.15
3	6.000%	466.37	76,582.11	6.000%	466.37	76,582.11
4	6.000%	466.37	76,498.65	6.000%	466.37	76,498.65
5	6.000%	466.37	76,414.77	6.000%	466.37	76,414.77
6	6.000%	466.37	76,330.47	6.000%	466.37	76,330.47
7	6.000%	466.37	76,245.75	6.000%	466.37	76,245.75
8	6.000%	466.37	76,160.61	6.000%	466.37	76,160.61
9	6.000%	466.37	76,075.04	6.000%	466.37	76,075.04
10	6.000%	466.37	75,989.05	6.000%	466.37	75,989.05
11	6.000%	466.37	75,902.63	6.000%	466.37	75,902.63
12	6.000%	466.37	75,815.77	6.000%	466.37	75,815.77
Year 1 Totals		$5,596.44			$5,596.44	
Cumulative Totals		$5,596.44			$5,596.44	

Month	Worst Case			Up Trend		
	ARM Rate	Payment	Balance	ARM Rate	Payment	Balance
13	8.000%	566.17	75,755.04	6.167%	474.37	75,731.01
14	8.000%	566.17	75,693.90	6.167%	474.37	75,645.81
15	8.000%	566.17	75,632.36	6.167%	474.37	75,560.18
16	8.000%	566.17	75,570.41	6.167%	474.37	75,474.11
17	8.000%	566.17	75,508.04	6.167%	474.37	75,387.59
18	8.000%	566.17	75,445.26	6.167%	474.37	75,300.63
19	8.000%	566.17	75,382.06	6.167%	474.37	75,213.22
20	8.000%	566.17	75,318.44	6.167%	474.37	75,125.36
21	8.000%	566.17	75,254.39	6.167%	474.37	75,037.05
22	8.000%	566.17	75,189.92	6.167%	474.37	74,948.29
23	8.000%	566.17	75,125.02	6.167%	474.37	74,859.07
24	8.000%	566.17	75,059.68	6.167%	474.37	74,769.39
Year 2 Totals		$6,794.04			$5,692.44	
Cumulative Totals		$12,390.48			$11,288.88	

	Worst Case			Up Trend		
Month	ARM Rate	Payment	Balance	ARM Rate	Payment	Balance
25	10.000%	671.11	75,014.07	8.167%	572.44	74,705.80
26	10.000%	671.11	74,968.08	8.167%	572.44	74,641.77
27	10.000%	671.11	74,921.70	8.167%	572.44	74,577.31
28	10.000%	671.11	74,874.94	8.167%	572.44	74,512.41
29	10.000%	671.11	74,827.79	8.167%	572.44	74,447.07
30	10.000%	671.11	74,780.24	8.167%	572.44	74,381.28
31	10.000%	671.11	74,732.30	8.167%	572.44	74,315.05
32	10.000%	671.11	74,683.96	8.167%	572.44	74,248.37
33	10.000%	671.11	74,635.22	8.167%	572.44	74,181.23
34	10.000%	671.11	74,586.07	8.167%	572.44	74,113.63
35	10.000%	671.11	74,536.51	8.167%	572.44	74,045.57
36	10.000%	671.11	74,486.54	8.167%	572.44	73,977.05
Year 3 Totals		$8,053.32			$6,869.28	
Cumulative Totals		$20,443.80			$18,158.16	

CHAPTER 10

Seller-Financing, Lease-to-Purchase, Contract for Deeds, & Options

It's funny, everything is so much easier when you do it yourself.
Picturequotes.com

SOMETIMES IT IS not your luck that determines your ability to reach a goal like buying your own home. It takes tenacity to push through brick walls, and ingenuity to maneuver around them.

Surrounding yourself with a team of professionals—who know the pitfalls—can also keep you out of harm's way, affording you the confidence to settle for no less than the best.

For many, non-traditional financing has been the answer to achieving homeownership when the credit, the bank account, and the property just did not meet the requirements of traditional government-backed loans and bank products.

Lease-to-Purchase is an agreement between the property owner and a tenant who agrees to purchase that property at a future date. The Lease-to-Purchase agreement contains a separate lease agreement showing the terms of the rental agreement and a contract signed at the time of the lease laying out the terms of the sale.

Lease-with-Option-to-Purchase agreement between the property owner and a tenant contains a separate lease agreement laying out the terms of rent, but the buyer would also pay an upfront Option payment which gives them the right to purchase the property for a specific price within a specific timeline. Since the buyer is signing an Option, he is not obligated to purchase, whereas the buyer would be obligated to purchase under the Lease-to-Purchase agreement.

There are advantages and disadvantages for both the property owner and the tenant using the Lease-to-Purchase and the Lease-with-Option-to-Purchase. Both the property owner who wishes to sell the property and the tenant who wishes to buy the property would be wise to consult a real estate attorney to work out the details.

Some of these contracts have expiry dates, specifying a period wherein the tenant-buyer must exercise his right to purchase the property at the set price. Some of these agreements require a large upfront deposit from the tenant-buyer with the understanding that the deposit cash will be used later toward the purchase with its amount reduced from the purchase price.

Most lease-to-purchase agreements set the amount of monthly rent. The contract spells out who takes on costs to maintain the home, and who pays the taxes and insurance. Some lease-to-purchase contracts include a clause that requires the owner-seller to credit back to the tenant-buyer a portion of the monthly rent toward down payment.

Mortgage regulations do not always allow this rent credit clause due to a limit on how much the seller can contribute toward the buyer's costs on the house sale. For example, the government FHA loan program restricts the seller's contributions toward the buyer's costs to 6% of the sale price or value, whichever is less.

The seller is allowed to contribute toward closing costs, prepaid taxes and insurance, and points to buy down the interest rate, but never allowed to contribute financially to the down payment.

With conventional programs, where the buyer pays less than 10% down, the seller can pay only up to 3% of the price or value, whichever is less.

Example:

Sale price:	$100,000
Minimum 3.5% down:	$3,500
Closing Costs:	$3,000
Prepaid Taxes and Insurance:	$2,500
Total Move-in Costs:	$9,000

If the lease-to-purchase contract stated that $300 of the total $1,000 rent each month over a two-year option period was to be credited back to the buyer on the day he closes on purchase of the home, then the seller will have exceeded the $6,000 limit on seller contributions for the sale.

Even if the rent credit of $300 × 24 months = $7,200 did *not* exceed the 6% limit, no contributions from the seller would be allowed to reduce the buyer's $3,500 down payment.

Some would argue that a portion of rent should qualify as credit toward earnest money; however, this could be thwarted by the appraisal not only of the home's purchase value, but also its rent value.

If the appraiser notes that market rent for the area is $900 per month, and this is *less* than the amount the tenant-buyer has been paying, then there is no room for the seller to allow a $100 per month rent credit because the tenant has been paying *less* than market rent.

Advantages to the buyer when using the lease-to-purchase method include the extended time frame to prepare for purchase. If the buyer needs to wait two years following bankruptcy before a mortgage company will approve him for a loan, then the lease-to-purchase agreement with a two-year option period will give him the time he needs to build back his credit and save money for the down payment or other costs that come with owning the home.

In a real estate market where the home values are going up, the buyer may be able to negotiate today's value on the home as the set price for his future purchase in two years. He may also negotiate that the full amount of his upfront deposit be applied like earnest money to the price of the home or other settlement costs. The upfront deposit he paid at the time of contract becomes a forced savings account that he can use for closing costs and down payment when his deposit money is returned at closing.

The buyer can unpack all of his belongings and hang all of his pictures on the wall when he moves in, even though he does not yet own the house. He knows that it is only a matter of time before the home will be his.

Advantages to the seller when using the lease-to-purchase method include immediate freedom from the burden and cost of upkeeping the home, and having other income to offset his own mortgage payment. If the market is slow and homes are taking long to sell, the seller may view the lease-to-own option as a quick way to financial relief. Other advantages include ...

... leasing to a tenant eager to make on-time rent ...

... while keeping the house in good condition.

The disadvantages of the lease-to-purchase method to the tenant-buyer include the reality of monthly payments without enjoying a title in his name. Until consummation of the sale, he can enjoy the home, but cannot acquire an equity line of credit secured on it for repairs or other family emergencies. He also has to trust that the owner-seller is keeping the mortgage, taxes, and insurance paid so that the home is not at risk of being foreclosed.

The disadvantages of the lease-to-purchase method to the owner-seller are the fact that he still owns the home and is responsible for his mortgage, taxes, and insurance. He has to trust that the tenant-buyer will not damage the property or abandon it in an unsaleable condition.

Dawn & Destiny

Mother and Daughter Cinch the Deal

Dawn had always considered herself a survivor. Trouble, trials, and tribulations had launched themselves at her throughout her life. Following a long, drawn-out, devastating divorce, Dawn felt too tired and beaten to climb out of the emotional and financial hole that seemed to trap her. Caring for her precious daughter Destiny is what compelled Dawn to take the next right step when nothing right seemed to be happening.

Before the divorce, Dawn's spouse had gone on several spending sprees with her credit cards. What savings she had squirreled away she spent on her divorce attorney. As if the financial betrayal wasn't bad enough, she found herself and her daughter abandoned without means to pay the mortgage.

Dawn was forced into bankruptcy and their home went into foreclosure.

Determined to survive at any cost, Dawn moved into a small apartment with cheap rent. Her days became consumed with caring for Destiny, going to work, getting Destiny from childcare, and late-night pondering how she might possibly own her own home again … where Destiny could play in her own backyard.

One afternoon, when Dawn went to get Destiny from childcare, she struck up a conversation with another mom. They both had been through divorces. When the lady discovered that Dawn was hoping buy a home close to her house, she remembered a neighbor who had to move out of town and needed to sell his home fast.

Dawn met with a mortgage loan officer and informed him of her previous foreclosure and bankruptcy. By then, the foreclosure was over a year old. The loan officer told Dawn to continue working on her credit for two more years. Thereafter, the bankruptcy should be seasoned enough for Dawn to qualify for a mortgage.

Dawn met with the seller, who had already moved out of town. They made an appointment with a real estate attorney who helped them put together a lease-to-purchase contract requiring Dawn to pay a set rent and keep the home in good condition.

The set house price reflected current market value of homes in the neighborhood, and Dawn agreed to consummate the purchase of the home in two years.

Dawn felt a thrill of victory pulse through her. The way ahead for Dawn and Destiny would have some twists and turns, but the journey was on the high road again.

The seller-financing method offers flexibility to buyer and seller, alike. The S.A.F.E. Act puts limits on the number of seller-financed transactions a home seller can do each year. Consult with your tax accountant and real estate attorney about the lending laws or tax consequences for seller-financing on the sale of a home.

Example of a creative seller-financed mortgage transaction:
Sale price: $175,000
Down Payment: 15% or $26,250
Amount the buyer-borrower *owes* the seller: $148,750

Interest Rate: 8%; Loan Term: payment amortized as a 30-year loan, but with full balance due and payable to the seller after 59 months.

Monthly Principal & Interest: $1,091
(borrower pays taxes and insurance separately)
Balloon Payment Due Month 60: $141,451.27

Buyer-borrower pays and seller *receives*:
Down Payment: $26,250
Total Interest (59 months): $58,000
Total Principal: $148,750
(including monthly increments over 59 months)
Total Payments to Seller: $233,000

The seller has a really good payday over 60 months on a house she sold for only $175,000.

Advantages of seller-financed loans to the buyer can vary. The buyer and seller have freedom with few restrictions on how they can craft the terms and create a win-win situation. There have been some instances when sellers have granted a one-year moratorium on payments, with the first payment not due until a year following purchase.

When *debt-to-income* ratios are too high, seller-financing can help the buyer if the buyer is self-employed and does not show enough income to qualify for a traditional mortgage. Other scenarios may occur during a divorce when the borrower has quitclaimed the house to their ex-spouse, but the ex-spouse has not made on-time payments, causing a traditional mortgage company to turn the borrower down since the mortgage is still in both the borrower's name and the ex-spouse's name. If the seller understands that the spouse and not the buyer is responsible for the default, then the seller can confidently offer to seller-finance the home to the buyer-borrower.

Appraisals showing needed repairs will not prevent the closing. Mortgage companies require certain repairs notated on the appraisal to be completed *before* closing. Such repairs include items affecting the structure, security, and sanitation of the home. The exception to this rule is when the buyer-borrower is getting a renovation and repair loan. The seller-financed note allows the borrower to buy the home *without* having to do the repairs before closing. The buyer can do them after closing over time if he chooses.

Disadvantage for the buyer on the owner-financed transaction is that the seller can skew the terms in his favor.

Higher Down Payment: In some cases, the seller demands a much higher down payment than the mortgage company would have required. Financing terms can vary greatly between buyer and seller when seller-financing is involved.

The interest rate, in some cases, is higher on the seller-financed note as compared to the rate offered by a standard mortgage company.

Balloon payments can be due a few years after the loan is originated, requiring the buyer-borrower to refinance with a standard bank or mortgage company to cover the balloon payment and meet the terms of the seller-financed loan.

Credit: Owner-financed notes usually do not get reported to the credit bureau and do not help the buyer-borrower build credit.

Do-It-Yourself: The buyer-borrower is responsible to pay appraisal and title fees. With transactions involving mortgage companies, strict rules require the mortgage company to order an appraisal through a government-approved Appraisal Management Company. On seller-financed notes, the buyer-borrower can order his own appraisal without strict regulations.

Advantages to the Seller can also vary from one transaction to another.

A Quick Closing can be a great advantage to the seller in a slow market.

More Profit over Time may turn out better for the seller because he gets the profit from the sale of his home, but he also gets the interest income that normally would have gone to the bank.

Capital Gains Delay: sellers should check with their tax professional and financial advisor to see if they have a lesser tax liability, or a delay in having to pay taxes on capital gains, when they take their profits in small increments instead of in one lump sum.

Easy Closing is another great possibility, especially if the seller is not required to make costly repairs before closing.

Partial liquidity if the seller needs quick cash: The seller's circumstances may change over time. If he suddenly needs a large lump sum, instead of waiting out the five years for the buyer to pay the note in full, investors can buy the seller's remaining payment stream at a discount.

For example, if there remains $143,000 owed on the mortgage, the new "note buyer" might offer something like $120,000 cash to buy the rights to the remaining income otherwise due the seller.

The seller would get $120,000 cash today, and the note buyer would receive all remaining payments plus the balloon payment.

The buyer-borrower would now be directed to make his payments to the note buyer instead of the seller.

Disadvantages of seller-financing to the seller include the risk of the buyer missing mortgage payments and costing the seller time plus legal fees to foreclose and repossess the property. There is also the risk that the property may not have been properly maintained and may require extensive repairs and expensive renovations before reselling it.

Contract for Deed—Buyer Beware: The contract for deed is also known as a "land contract." Consult with a real estate attorney and financial advisor before entering into an agreement such as this one. Even though the contract for deed is similar to the seller-financing scenario, there are significant differences.

Unlike in seller-financing, with contract for deed, the title remains in the seller's name until all payments are made—in full.

At times, there are clauses in these agreements that can cause the buyer to lose his right to the property because of one or two late payments. That can be a grievous loss to the buyer, especially if she has been making payments for years and come close to the end of contract only to lose her title rights.

Resources

Consult with your local real estate attorney.

Consult with your licensed financial advisor.

CHAPTER 11

Renovation and Repair Loans

Renovating old homes is not about making them look new ...
It is about making new unnecessary.

Ty McBride

SOME OF MY mortgage clients over the years have been innovative and gutsy. They set their minds on what they want for their home and how much they will pay for it. If they cannot find the house that meets their needs in the neighborhood where they want to live, they will just rehab, repair, or modify it to make it what they want and need. At the right price and with the right team of professionals, nothing is impossible for these motivated clients.

The FHA 203(k) Renovation and Repair Loan —Buy Low, Add Value

If the perfect house for you is a home that is beaten up and needs repairs, the FHA 203(k) Renovation and Repair loan program may be the perfect pick for you.

The 203(k) loan program is used for financing 1-4 unit, owner-occupied homes that need remodeling or repairing. This loan allows the buyer to finance the cost of the house along with the cost to repair it.

Standard FHA 203(k) loan is used for structural and smaller repairs and renovations, but does not provide financing for luxury items. This program requires a HUD Consultant to be assigned by the mortgage company to ensure costs are in line with industry standards, and that the work is completed by a licensed contractor in a workmanlike fashion. To be eligible, total repair cost must exceed $5,000.

Ineligible repairs:
- Swimming pools (unless repairing an existing pool)
- Exterior barbecue, fireplace pits, exterior tubs, spas, saunas
- Gazeboes
- Alterations to serve a commercial use of the property
- And more …

Eligible repairs:
- Add a room or living space
- Foundation repairs
- Other standard repairs and renovations, not including luxury items

The HUD consultant inspects the home periodically whenever a draw from the repair escrow fund is requested. The consultant checks to make sure the work was done according to cost estimates in a workmanlike manner.

The borrower is not allowed to perform repairs and renovations, but there are exceptions to this rule in the FHA guidelines.

Limited FHA 203(k) loan is used for minor remodeling and repairs that do not include any structural repairs, luxury items, or modifications for commercial use. Total cost of repair items cannot exceed $35,000 dollars. A HUD Consultant is not required to monitor the project.

A licensed contractor, and not the borrower, must complete the work on the home. There are some exceptions in the FHA guidelines allowing the borrower to complete some of the work. When the cost estimates exceed $35,000, a licensed general contractor may be required depending on the scope of the work.

The 203(k) Standard and limited programs require hired contractors to be licensed and approved by the mortgage company. There are several disclosures the contractor will need to review and sign, spelling out the process until completion of work.

If the transaction involves a home purchase, the home purchase sale contract must specify that the loan program is an FHA 203(k) renovation and repair loan. Due to the amount of paperwork on the Standard program and the time it takes to get appraisal, approval on the contractor's cost estimates, and other loan documents processed, no less than 45 to 60 days is suggested from the offer acceptance to the day of closing.

The appraiser gives two different valuations on the appraisal: the "as-is value" as the house sits without repairs and renovations; and the "after-repaired value" (ARV). FHA will allow the base loan amount to go up to 110% of the ARV on the home.

Advantages of the FHA 203(k) Loan Programs

The FHA renovation and repair loans allow a seller to sell a property without having to invest his own funds into home repairs before he gets the funds from the sale at closing.

The buyer can pick up a bargain property, in some cases, and finance the costs of repairs without having to spend his own savings.

The realtor can get paid her commission at the closing table since the title goes into the buyer's name and the repairs are completed later.

Many times, the advantage of getting the renovation and repair loan is that you can buy the house at a much lower price, finance the repairs, and hopefully end up with a house that is worth far more than youhave invested in it.

Disadvantages of the FHA 203(k) Loan Program

The FHA renovation and repair loans take longer to close because it takes time to get genuine and detailed quotes from the contractor. Once the buyer selects a contractor, the mortgage company must then review the contractor for approval.

Costs tend to be higher when the buyer is getting an FHA 203(k) loan. The interest rate is usually higher than market mortgage rates, often by about a half of one percent on the price of the rate. The closing costs are also higher due to the inspection fees throughout the repair process, and the costs to update the home's title at each inspection. This is done to ensure no contractor has filed any mechanic's liens on the property. For loans that require the HUD Consultant to be assigned, hiring the consultant adds an additional fee.

Steps in the Process

Once your home purchase contract has been accepted by the seller, it is time to start moving through the loan process.

1. Get an itemized quote for home repairs from a licensed contractor.
2. The mortgage company will request a HUD Consultant to be assigned to the case.
3. Meet with the HUD Consultant and licensed contractor at the house to review the list of repairs.
4. The HUD Consultant reviews the estimate and determines the official repair costs for the mortgage company to use when calculating the mortgage amount.
5. The HUD Consultant works out with the contractor which group of repairs will need to be completed before the next draw can be taken from the escrow table to fund that segment of the job.
6. The mortgage company orders a 203(k) appraisal, title work, and begins the process of approving the contractor(s).
7. The mortgage company works with the borrower to get their loan fully approved.
8. The loan closes and the title is now in the buyer's name; repair costs that are included in the mortgage are placed in a repair escrow account.
9. The renovation and repair work now begins. As each predetermined stage of repairs is completed, the contractor requests a draw for that portion to be paid. The title company orders a title update at each draw. The HUD Consultant completes an inspection of that segment of completed repairs.
10. When the home is completed, any money left in the repair escrow will be applied to reduce the balance on the borrower's loan.

Example of an FHA 203(k) Loan Transaction

The Lancaster Family

The Price Is Right When You Renovate

Some of the best bargain real estate deals involve properties with repair problems and other issues that snag traditional mortgage financing.

For homebuyers seeking a primary residence that needs $5,000 up to more than $100,000 in repairs—the FHA 203(k) Renovation Repair loan or the conventional HomeStyle Renovation and Repair loan can help the homebuyer finance the house and all or most of the repairs with one loan.

The move-in cost in this scenario is usually a little higher than with a regular mortgage, but may still qualify for a low 3.5% to 10% down, depending on which rehab loan product is used.

The mortgage rate is fixed and fairly low, keeping mortgage payments low, even though the interest rate for renovation and repair loans is usually about a quarter to a half percent higher than the rates for mortgages without repair loans.

Mr. and Mrs. Lancaster found a house in the country close to other family members. It had a perfect layout for enjoying their retirement, complete with a bonus room for visiting grandchildren. The property was priced well below the other homes, making it affordable to the Lancasters on their retirement income. It was truly a needle in a haystack; but it did have some flaws.

The house had rotted wood that needed to be replaced and painted; the bonus room needed finishing to make it a livable space; and the electrical system needed a few fixes.

The Lancaster family found themselves in a catch-22. The mortgage company would not allow them to close on the home until the repairs were done, but they couldn't make the repairs until they owned the house.

The solution? An FHA 203(k) Renovation and Repair loan.

Factoring both the house sale price and the cost of the repairs, the home was still worth quite a bit more than they had to spend. With an FHA Renovation and Repair loan, the Lancasters earned their celebration day and bragging rights at closing when they went home to their new digs.

Take a look at the structure on the Lancasters' FHA 203(k) loan:

Sale price		$100,000
Repair costs		$ 38,000
Reserve on repairs		$ 7,600
HUD Consultant		$ 600
5 inspections during renovation project	$175 x 5=	$ 875
5 title updates to clear any liens	$175 x 5=	$ 875
Total renovation costs		$ 47,950

Sale price $100,000 + renovation costs $47,950	= **$147,950**
Down payment = (Total costs $147,950 x 3.5%)	= **$ 5,178**

FHA 203(k) total loan amount is: sale price plus renovation costs minus down payment—$147,950 – $5,178 = $143,772

The Lancasters' pay at closing:

Down payment:	+$5,178
Regular closing costs (without renovation costs):	+$4,000
Prepaid taxes and insurance:	+$3,500
Seller's $6,000 contribution toward closing costs:	**–$6,000**
Total move-in costs on closing day	**$6,678**

As-is appraised value: $105,000
After-repaired value: $190,000

With FHA loans, a 1.75% upfront mortgage insurance fee is tacked onto the base loan so that the borrower does not have to pay this fee in cash.

$143,772 base loan amount × 1.0175 = $146,288

The final loan amount with upfront mortgage insurance added to the base loan comes to $146,288.

The Conventional Renovation and Repair Loan is very much like the FHA 203(k) except that the conventional version offers renovation and repair loans to both owner-occupants using the home as their primary residence, *and also* real estate investors not occupying the property as their primary residence.

The minimum down payment for the owner-occupants purchasing the property as their primary residence is 5% plus renovation costs, very similar to the FHA version. For investors, a minimum 10% down payment is required.

The conventional and FHA renovation and repair loans also differ concerning luxury items. For instance, whereas the conventional loan would allow a homeowner to use the renovation money to build a new swimming pool, the FHA 203(k) would not.

Resources

203(k) loan guideline: https://www.hud.gov/sites/documents/40001HSGH. PDF

Fannie Mae HomeStyle Renovation: https://singlefamily.fanniemae.com/ originating-underwriting/mortgage-products/homestyle-renovation

CHAPTER 12

Mortgages for Real Estate Investors

Ninety percent of all millionaires became so through owning real estate.

Andrew Carnegie

Reasons to Buy Real Estate

IF I ASKED everyone reading this chapter why they are interested in buying real estate, each person would have a different angle; but, when you sift through to the core, most want two things: to earn extra income and build wealth.

To be successful in real estate investment, you need a detailed vision of how you will launch and sustain your venture to those dreamed-of profits.

If you'd like to avoid taking expensive "seminars" through costly mistakes, engage your local real estate investor association. Connect regularly with people who have already established a successful track record and a real estate portfolio. Take classes on real estate financing through your local association or from adult continuing education classes. Learn your options for issues you'll face such as tenant screening, property management, and special financing. Connect with successful real estate investors, take them to lunch, and get their advice when you need to make a decision. Chances are good they've made a few mistakes, and learning from *their mistakes* will be much easier than learning from your own.

Raymond Ridley

Work Smarter Not Harder

Owning your own home can bring joy and satisfaction in so many ways having nothing to do with money. A home is your castle. It is the neighborhood where your children grow up, where family memories are made and are retold for years during family gatherings. These things are priceless ... but the financial benefits can be great, too.

Raymond Ridley, a licensed real estate broker and full-time investor, has successfully owned, rehabbed, and sold over 500 homes and apartment units. Raymond started out as a hard-working, money-making realtor, but having to shovel half of his earnings over to Uncle Sam for taxes wasn't his cup of tea.

Working harder was not the answer. He had to figure out how to work *smarter.*

Raymond told a bunch of fellow realtors and investors, "I have probably made more money in real estate than anyone in this room, and I have probably lost more money in real estate than anyone in this room. When someone earns an hourly wage, he has to be on the job every day to earn his pay. When he builds wealth by buying real estate, the tenants pay him rents—even when he is on vacation."

Raymond presented six reasons to enjoy investing in real estate:

1. Cash flow on a rental property is equal to the monthly income minus the mortgage payment including taxes and insurance. (So: Income – PITI = Cash Flow.)

   If you plan to keep the rental house a long time, the 30-year fixed-rate mortgage is a great tool. With a 30-year mortgage, you enjoy a principal and interest payment that stays the same for the life of the loan. This means that every rent increase affords you a pay raise. While the rent goes up, your payments stay the same, which gives you a bigger and better margin.

2. Appreciation is the rate that the house value increases every year. Raymond pointed out that there is a direct correlation between positive cash flow and appreciation. Cash flow is usually less per month in areas with higher appreciation rates. For example, real estate investors who buy homes in areas that are going up in value faster compared to other areas usually pay a higher price with a smaller profit each month on rent income.

   Investors can usually pay less for homes in areas that are not appreciating in value. Rents tend to increase at a faster pace than home prices, which typically brings increased positive monthly cash flow to the investor.

3. Real estate can provide a wonderful tax shelter enabling an investor to make a six-figure income and pay zero taxes*. Raymond confessed that sheltering almost all of his income was where he learned to work smarter and not harder.

   To shelter $50,000 per year in income, an investor would need approximately $1,000,000 in real estate. Raymond prefers having ten houses valued at about $100,000 over 30 houses valued at $30,000. With ten houses, he has only ten tenants and ten potential dramas, which sounds a lot better than 30 tenants with a potential 30 problems.

4. Thanks to amortization, with each mortgage payment the principal balance is paid down at a faster pace. The investor builds equity on the house as the mortgage is paid off. Later, the investor may choose to borrow against this equity to purchase another property.

5. The fifth advantage of owning real estate is leverage. Real estate is one of the few investments that allows the investor to borrow almost the entire value of the investment without a large lump sum of cash.

6. Last but not least: investing in real estate opens opportunity for family relationship bonding while working together in the investment business.

Raymond illustrated with his own example of profits on a $100,000 house:

Amortization: $100 per month
Positive cash flow: $200 per month
Tax Shelter: $300 per month

Appreciation: $200 per month
Total: $800 per month
This comes to approximately $10,000 in profits yearly per house.

Common Types of Financing for Investment Properties

If you look hard enough, you will find the thing you seek. This holds true not only for house-hunting but as well for discovering the best financing for your income-producing real estate. Choices come in a wide range including traditional long-term, fixed low-rate programs; loans from untraditional sources; and loans secured on other assets and homes that you own.

Conventional Mortgage or Bank Loan

If you are planning to hold onto the income-producing property for a while, the conventional or standard bank loan may be your best financing option. The fixed-rate, stable, traditional mortgage allows the borrower to enjoy a fixed P&I payment for up to 30 years. As the rent income increases the P&I payment stays the same. The growing margin between the mortgage payment and the rising rent creates an increasing positive cash flow to the investor.

Properties Financed

Under the current guidelines at the time of this writing, there is no limit to the number of financed properties a borrower can own when the property is a *primary* residence; however, there is a restriction on the number of financed *rental* properties the borrower can own.

Fannie Mae allows a borrower to own up to 10 ten financed real estate properties, including the loan he is applying to get when he is purchasing or refinancing an investment property. The maximum 10-financed-property rule works when the lender uses automated underwriting software. The borrower may be limited to owning up to six financed properties instead of 10 if the mortgage is manually underwritten. When refinancing to pull cash out of an investment property, the number of financed properties the investor is allowed to own is reduced even more.

Qualified income amounts from rental properties vary depending on the loan product. If the borrower has been using a particular property as rental income for over a year, the net income with some adjustments is calculated from tax returns. For a newly acquired rental property on which one has yet to file a tax return, the mortgage company calculates rental income as 75% of the gross rent.

Rates for mortgages and refinancing loans tend to be higher on investment properties than on a primary residence. Depending on the mortgage market nuances, the mortgage rate offered for the purchase or refinance of a real estate investment is .5% or .75% higher than that for a primary residence.

If the buyer is putting less than 20% down, the borrower will be paying for the lender's private mortgage insurance, which is usually higher for investment loans.

Private Mortgage Insurance reduces the lender's risk, enabling them to offer the borrower less than 20% down. As the investor, your goal is to pay the least amount possible for private mortgage insurance.

Money Down requirements are higher than for primary residences when purchasing or refinancing an income-producing property.

Example: Single-Family Primary Residence, 5% Standard Conventional Loan

Sale price:	$200,000
Down payment: 5% or	$10,000
Closing cost:	~$4,000
Prepaid taxes and insurance:	~$3,500
Total =	$17,500

Sellers are allowed to pay up to 3% of the sale price toward the buyer's closing cost if these terms are negotiated into the home purchase contract: $17,500 – $6,000 = $11,500

Example: Single-Family Investment Property, 15% to 20% Down

Sale price:	$200,000
Down payment: 15% or $30,000 to 20% or	$40,000
Closing costs:	~$4,000
Prepaid taxes and insurance:	$3,500
Total =	$47,500

Sellers are allowed to pay up to 2% of the sale price toward the buyer's closing cost if these terms are negotiated into the home purchase contract: $47,500 - $4,000 = $43,500

Example of Investment Duplex to 4-plex Investment Rental Property, 25% Minimum Down

Sale price:	$200,000
Down payment:	$50,000
Closing costs:	$3,500
Prepaid taxes and insurance:	$3,500
Total =	$57,000

Sellers are allowed to pay up to 2% of the sale price toward the buyer's closing costs if these terms are negotiated into the home purchase contract: $57,000 – $4,000 = $53,000

Reserves are the extra money left in savings after down payment and other costs are paid at the closing table.

Traditional mortgage regulations require the borrower to show adequate money available after closing. Required reserve amounts vary from one loan program to another. At the time of this writing, if the borrower owned three financed properties, Fannie Mae guidelines would require 2% of the unpaid balances on the mortgages secured in reserves for these properties; if six, it would increase to 4%; if eight, required reserves would increase to 6%.

On a different loan program, the lender might calculate the required reserves by adding up eight months' worth of house payments on each financed property. The unpaid balance on a primary residence is not included in the required reserve calculation.

Currently, there are no restrictions on the number of homes a person can own without financing. A real estate investor could own twelve or more properties free and clear. Only those which are secured with loans are subject to limitations.

Second homes or vacation homes do not generate any rental income. Mortgage underwriting guidelines only allow financing on a second home that is located over 75 miles away from the owner's primary residence. There are exceptions to the 75-mile radius when the vacation home is located in a known resort area. Homes that qualify as non-income generating second homes require only a minimum down payment of 10% with a mortgage interest rate much closer to the low mortgage rates for primary residences.

Niles Nelson

Slow and Sure

The most popular and well-known mortgage product for the investor looking to rent to tenants is the 30-year fixed-rate. These typically invest a 20% down payment with some closing costs added. The interest rate on the 30-year investment loan is about 1% or so higher than the rate for primary residence.

Let Niles Nelson show you what a first-time real estate investor can do. Niles owned his own home but wanted to start slowly with investing in real estate until he could learn the ropes.

Niles found a house in a stable neighborhood. He researched Craig's List and consulted his realtor to confirm that the area supported a strong rental market, with rents increasing about 5% per year, on average. Niles paid around $114,000—not a bargain price since the value came in around $115,000.

He got excellent terms through a 30-year fixed rate with 20% down. The P&I payment that would never increase was about $455/month. With taxes and insurance, the total payment was around $630/month. As for rent income, Niles was getting a check in his mailbox every month for $1,195/month. He had an almost instant positive cash flow of about $600 per month. Rents were going up about 5% per year and Niles figured the following year or two he could raise the rent to enjoy a $900/month positive cash flow.

Words to the wise on the standard mortgage programs:

Be sure you save some of the positive cash flow because, as you continue to buy investment properties, you will have to show more reserves to prove to lenders that you can weather unexpected expenses on your real estate properties.

Niles could have put down as little as 15% if he was okay with paying a little private mortgage insurance. If he was short on down payment funds, he could have borrowed against his 401(k) or used funds from the home equity line of credit on his primary residence.

On investment loans, the borrower is allowed a maximum of ten *financed* properties in his or her name, or a lot more than ten without financing—not including commercial buildings. Because of this maximum financed property rule, Niles planned to get about eight properties over time and eventually pull some of the equity from a few of them to pay off the rest so he could enjoy 30-year fixed rates on yet more investment properties.

It is also possible for an investor to enjoy the benefits of a cash-out refinance provided they meet the six-month seasoning requirement. This requirement on the traditional 15-, 20-, or 30-year mortgage means the buyer-investor must own the property for at least six months before they are eligible for the cash-out refinance. However, there is a way around this and it is, as you would expect, a popular mortgage product for investors. I call it the Quick Cash Back Refinance.

In a quick cash back refinance, the six-month seasoning requirement is waived and cash becomes available when an investor purchases a "fixer-upper" and completes all repairs in a shorter time frame.

A popular mortgage strategy with my clients recently has been to refinance their homes to include paying off debt from variable-rate credit cards and the variable rate Home Equity Line of Credit. Most of these homeowners had acquired quite a bit of variable rate debt because of unexpected family needs or other emergencies.

Hard Money Loans and Private Funding

Some of the most popular private financing types are seller-financing and the hard money loan. Other strategies for acquiring investment real estate are lease-to-own and the contract for deed.

Hard money lenders usually provide funds for a short time with a high-interest rate. The advantage of hard money is a quick closing in one or two weeks as compared to a month with traditional financing. Hard money usually finances both the home purchase *and* the renovation and repair costs.

Seller-financing usually occurs when the seller owns a property free and clear and lends his *equity* to the buyer. No mortgage funding happens at closing. The buyers usually pay the seller five to twenty percent of the sale price as down payment, followed by regular monthly payments until the entire loan is paid off. The advantage to both buyer and seller is that neither has to jump through hoops to qualify under a bank or mortgage company's strict regulations. The seller can always sell all or part of his income stream to a note buyer if he needs cash in the future.

Contracts for deed transactions are risky for a buyer entering into the contract, depending on the terms. The home buyer usually does not get his name on the property title until he has paid the entire mortgage balance. If the buyer misses a payment, the owner can cancel the contract for deed and repossess the home, causing the buyer to lose their buying right. Check with a real estate attorney before engaging in a contract using these instruments.

Getting the Deal Closed Using Hard Money Lenders

Douglas Drewman was already a successful real estate investor and rehabber from the Memphis area when he got a call from someone ready to sell a multi-unit property at a cut-rate price. The deal was too good to let go, but Douglas had a big problem. He and his family were going out of state the next day on a much-needed week-long vacation. To grab this deal, Douglas had to arrive at the closing table with cash the day after he returned.

A good number of people would resign themselves to kissing this sweet deal good-bye … but Douglas had a plan. He punched in the number for private lender Audrey Akerman, also known as "The Mortgage Lady." It didn't take long for Douglas to give Audrey the details of the deal including the value, cost to repair, and the projected profit once the property was completely rehabbed.

Audrey did a quick check on the property value and repair costs. She already had credit and background checks on Douglas from previous transactions. Her last words to Douglas before he left town went something like this, "Go have a great time on your vacation, Doug. I'll have the money ready for your closing when you return."

These quick money lenders are sometimes pictured as sinister hoodlums lurking in dark alleys waiting to break borrower's kneecaps when they can't repay. However, professional hard money lenders are NOT the mob, but they are not the mama either. Interest rates can go well into the double digits with upfront points depending on the risk factors.

Generally, the hard money loan is a temporary loan until the borrower can secure permanent financing or another method. The main differences between a professional hard money lender like Audrey Akerman and an unscrupulous predatory lender are the design of the loan terms and the type of borrower. The unscrupulous lender structures the loan so that borrowers inevitably fail and the lender/predator can take the house in foreclosure. On the other hand, the professional hard money lender structures reasonable terms because he wants *his money and fees*—not the borrower's house.

There are probably as many different hard money lending loan terms as there are hard money transactions. Douglas Drewman and Audrey Akerman's loan structure looked something like this:

The sale price on "AS IS" multi-unit: ....under $ 20,000
Cost to repair property: ....$ 50,000
Value of property "AS IS" ....$ 108,000
Hard Money Loan 65% LTV: ....$ 70,200
Points paid: .... $ 7,200
(by Douglas to "The Mortgage Lady" at time of payoff,
plus interest paid monthly)
Term of hard money loan: 6 months
Douglas' PROFIT at the end of the deal: !!!!!$ 60,000 !!!!!

Hard money lenders fill a niche in mortgage lending, helping consumers who have specialized needs. They can be found all over the United States and the world.

Another technique for a no-money-down purchase of a rental property normally requiring a 15% or 20% down payment is to finance with other assets the buyer owns.

Financing to Buy a Home with Funding Secured on a Different Asset

There are many cases and situations for a home buyer seeking funding secured on a different asset. Sometimes, the home the buyer wants is in such poor condition that their security asset just doesn't cut it for the lender.

If the home she wants to buy is selling for $100,000, she might get a loan secured on her retirement fund; she might use a 2nd mortgage credit line secured on her primary residence; or, she might explore any of many other options. Other typical assets used to fund purchase of a rental property include:

Places to Look for Funds

- Cash value on life insurance
- Cash-out refinance on a different real estate property the buyer owns
- Margin loan on stocks and bonds
- Business loan
- A loan from a family member
- Municipal grants and special financing for target areas
- Seller financing
- Home equity line of credit secured on a different property

Barry

The Investor & the Investor's Grandkids

Barry had a life dream of not having to work a job so he could spend quality time with his wife and children and, later, his grandchildren.

Before he had that vision clearly defined, he really didn't pursue it. With efforts relegated to after-work hours and early Saturday mornings, it was hard for him to find the energy to venture out, search, and negotiate with sellers. Investment real estate is hard work.

After a while, Barry accepted the fact that good rental home deals just wouldn't fall in his lap. Reflecting on how desperately he desired to give his family the life of *their* dreams, his hunger for the dream came fully alive. He finally had his WHY to power him forward.

What do you want *your* life to look like? How many daily hours do you want to devote to work, and what do you want your work environment to look like in the future? What kind of income do you want? Is your WHY big enough to compel you to do the day in day out tasks that will propel you to your dream? *If your WHY is big enough, you can do anything!*

Once Barry found his WHY, he committed. Now he's buying two to three rental properties per year. He looks for fixer-uppers and buys them at bargain prices. To buy them with cash, he uses either the equity line on his primary residence or a line of credit secured on another owned property. The seller usually is more willing to sell at a bargain price because Barry is self-financing with cash, eliminating the need to wait for an appraisal before closing.

At closings, Barry is a happy investor and he's got a plan. With keys just in hand, he heads straight to the house with his fix-it-up crew. Usually in a matter of weeks, Barry's bargain house is fixed, painted, and ready for his new happy tenants to move in and start paying him rent.

Since I am Barry's mortgage officer, he and I work together a lot. Going in to a deal, I already know he wants to pay his variable credit line back as soon as possible and get his low fixed-rate 30-year mortgage in place. Before Barry even closes on a house, he and I have started processing his loan request for the long-term fixed-rate mortgage. By the time Barry has driven the last nail and painted the last wall in the house, I have done an appraisal for his permanent loan and gotten him approved.

Closing on the fixed low-interest 30-year mortgage, he pays off the credit lines used to purchase the home. Once his credit lines are paid off, more credit becomes available to make his next bargain purchase.

Supporting Documents to Give Your Traditional Lender

1. ALL PAGES of your last two years' tax returns. If you are self-employed and own over 25% of a business, include the last two years' corporate or partnership tax returns on all pages including any K-1s. In some cases, a year-to-date Profit & Loss statement may be required.

   You must disclose any payment plans made to IRS or other outside agreements that may not show on the credit report. These payments need to be calculated to determine your true DTI ratio.

   If your IRS transcripts or tax returns indicate that taxes are owed, you must document the source of funds to clear the taxes owed or show proof of accepted payment plan and proof of three months' payments made to IRS or other agency to clear the debt.

2. ALL W-2 and 1099 forms that go with the last two years' tax returns plus those received in January of the latest year.
3. Latest paystubs (two).
4. ALL PAGES of the last two months' bank statements and investment accounts.
5. Legible copy of your driver's license(s).
6. Name and contact info for your chosen homeowners insurance agency that will cover the property.
7. A signed and dated letter explaining the status of any inquiries appearing on the credit report to state whether or not a new account was opened. If a new account was opened as a result of an inquiry on the credit report, all pages of the latest statement for that account must be submitted.
8. Divorce decree and martial dissolution agreement/child support documentation if applicable.

If you receive retirement income:

9. Submit all pages of the latest entitlement letter from social security or other pension or retirement fund.

If you own rental real estate property:

10. All pages of leases on properties.
11. A declaration page from your insurance company on each property verifying coverage, premium amount, and next due date, and if there are any liens on the property.
12. Copy of municipal/county tax record showing the amount of real estate property taxes levied to each rental property.
13. Verification of association fees if there are any on any of the rental properties.
14. Latest mortgage statements on each applicable property.
15. All pages of closing disclosures showing the sale or purchase of any real estate properties transferred after the last reported tax year.

In case you are refinancing a home:

16. Include a copy of all the mortgage or lien statements secured on that property.
17. Make sure your home has not been listed for sale within the last six months.

Resources

National Real Estate Investors Association (REIA): https://nationalreia.org/

Fannie Mae underwriting guidelines https://singlefamily.fanniemae.com/ originating-underwriting

Freddie Mac underwriting guidelines https://sf.freddiemac.com/ working-with-us/origination-underwriting/mortgage-products

www.smarterlandlording.com Good info on property management

*Consult with your certified financial advisor.

CHAPTER 13

Reverse Mortgages

Respect your elders and the world will respect you.
The Random Vibe

WHAT IF I told you we could make your home pay YOU? Have you considered a reverse mortgage? If you are over 62 years old, maybe you should.

The reverse mortgage program is available to borrowers 62 and up. It's called a "reverse" mortgage because it acts "in reverse" from other programs. Instead of the *borrower* paying the mortgage company, the *mortgage company* makes payments to the borrower.

Borrowers applying for the reverse mortgage must complete a HUD-approved Reverse Mortgage Counseling session. You can find a reverse mortgage counselor by calling 1-800-569-4287 or going to **www. hud.gov**

Three Types of Reverse Mortgages

The Private Reverse Mortgage is handled through a bank or other lender that tailors their own program guidelines with fewer restrictions than government-backed programs. Borrowers can usually borrow more money, but may also pay higher fees.

The Single-Purpose Reverse Mortgage is usually offered by non-profit organizations or by local municipal government agencies. It is so-named because this type of reverse mortgage is only allowed for funding certain expenses. Examples would include home improvements or to pay property taxes.

The Home Equity Conversion Mortgage (HECM) is a government-insured loan backed by the Federal Housing Administration (FHA). The borrower enjoys lower fees on this type of reverse mortgage since the government limits how much a lender can charge. There are more payment options available on the HECM program than on any other type.

The following are payment types currently available on the HECM:

A. Line of Credit—used only when you want or need to use it.

B. Term Payment—the borrower sets up a monthly payment for a specified time. For example, when a 65-year-old borrower needs income but does not want to initiate social security for five more years, they can set up the reverse mortgage to pay them a fixed amount every month for that five years. The reverse mortgage effectively buys them time during which their social security will increase, resulting in higher monthly social security checks once initiated.

C. Tenure payment—the reverse mortgage payment provides the borrower with fixed payments for as long as the borrower lives in the home as primary residence. If the payments received by the borrower from the reverse mortgage lender exceed the value on the home, the borrower would continue to receive the payments.

D. Modified Term/Line of Credit—sets up a line of credit and the borrower receives a fixed income as long as he or she lives in the home as their primary residence.

E. Single Disbursement—this program is used when the borrower buys a home. Sometimes borrowers want to sell their existing home and downsize to a smaller or different one. When this happens, the borrower can get a single disbursement lump sum to pay cash for the new home enabling them to live in the new home with no mortgage payment.

Advantages of Using the Reverse Mortgage

The reverse mortgage program does not work well for everyone. It can be a godsend for house-rich-cash-poor borrowers over 62 years of age that own their home free and clear, or have 75% equity available. If the borrower has other assets that can be reallocated to create an income, usually that route is better than a reverse mortgage.

Here is an example where the reverse mortgage allowed a borrower to remain safely and contentedly in her home.

Opal Osborn

A Timely Reversal

Let's start with Opal Osborn's story. Mrs. Osborn's husband of 50 years had passed away leaving her with less income and little money; nevertheless, Mrs. Osborn was far from empty-handed as she still owned a $175,000 home ... free and clear.

Mrs. Osborn's son called me after listening to Real Estate Mortgage Shoppe and told me his mother wanted desperately to continue living in her home, but needed money to make repairs.

After a bit of digging, we were able to get Mrs. Osborn approved for a reverse mortgage where she got a portion of the money upfront for the needed repairs, and then continued to receive monthly payments from the reverse mortgage program. The reverse mortgage was a God-send for her.

Carter and Claire Caldwell

Bounding over Barriers to Be with Grandbabies

If you want to see *stunningly brilliant* strategy, observe what happens when grandparents are determined to spring themselves across the miles to hold their grandbabies in their laps.

Carter and Claire Caldwell were both over 62 years old. They loved their primary home next to the lake, their longstanding neighbors and friends, and wanted to continue living in their primary residence most of the year; however, the Caldwells also yearned to spend time playing with their toddler grandchildren who lived several hundred miles away. These grandparents were motivated to financially mastermind a second home near their grandkids.

Being over 62 and with their mortgage paid off early, the Caldwells applied and got approved for a Reverse Mortgage on their primary residence. Reverse mortgages cannot be used on second homes or investment properties.

The Reverse Mortgage on their *primary* residence was now paying *them* each month enough money to make the *second home* affordable … achieving their dream of enjoying five months at a time in the same town playing and making memories with their grandkids.

Disadvantages of the Reverse Mortgage

Rarely is a reverse mortgage the best deal for the borrower or for their family members. The reverse mortgage is expensive and eats up their equity. While the borrower enjoys receiving monthly income from the lender, the equity left for children or other heirs is greatly reduced.

The reverse mortgage program requires that the borrower live in the home for a certain number of months out of the year. If the borrower needs to go into a care facility and cannot occupy the primary residence to continue qualifying *as* a primary residence, then comes payback time and the house must be sold or the mortgage repaid to the lender.

This is a possible reverse mortgage payback scenario:

A borrower takes out a reverse mortgage for $300,000 on a house valued at $500,000. After she passes away, the family sells the house for $600,000, but the mortgage pay-off is now $450,000. The profit left for the heirs is only $150,000.

Consult with a HUD-approved reverse mortgage counselor and check terms with reputable reverse mortgage lenders.

Funds for the Heirs to Keep the Home

There are several possible solutions for keeping the "family house" in the family. The first step is for the family members to consult with their CPA and certified financial advisor.

The reverse mortgage borrower could buy a term life insurance policy for enough to cover the reverse mortgage on their death, allowing the home to stay in the family.

Other family members can work together to pool family funds and pay off the reverse mortgage. These funds could be in the form of cash or a loan secured on other assets like stocks and bonds, credit lines, cash-out mortgages on other homes, and more.

Resources

https://www.hud.gov/program_offices/housing/sfh/hecm/hecmhome
   The government HUD site with information about the reverse mortgage loan program and a list of HUD-approved Reverse Mortgage Counselors

CHAPTER 14

Combo, Construction, Blanket, Bridge, and Bank Loans

The desire of gold is not for gold. It is for the means of freedom and benefit.

Ralph Waldo Emerson

VALUABLE FRIENDS LIKE valuable coins come in handy when you are in a pinch, especially if your banker is also one of your friends.

Over the years, mortgage customers have told me their stories that could have ended in disaster if not for a friend at the bank. Bank loans are varied and can help bridge the gap if the mortgage customer cannot qualify for a mortgage loan at the moment they need it. Temporary bank loans and "piggyback seconds" have saved more than a few real estate closings.

Bank loans come in a wide variety, with some secured on assets, including business assets, a car, or stocks and bonds. On the other hand, some are not secured at all as in the case of a signature loan or credit card. In this chapter, we explore bank loans that are secured on real estate. If the borrower doesn't pay, the bank, like the mortgage company, will foreclose and take back the property.

Bank loans tend to have a shorter term than traditional mortgages, and boast more flexibility on how their terms are structured. Traditional mortgages usually have a fixed interest rate for 10, 15, 20, 25, or 30 years. Some mortgages offer adjustable-rate mortgage terms, but the index, and annual and lifetime caps on the adjustable-rate programs are clearly set in place. Banks have regulations, too, but enjoy more flexibility to design their programs freely. Be aware: bank terms may *not* be as desirable to the borrower over a long period of time.

When a borrower purchases a home with intent to own for over five years, she knows the set terms on the mortgage. The mortgage company will not be calling her and demanding payment in full before the maturity date unless the borrower has violated terms of the mortgage or deed of trust agreement. The mortgage rate is usually fixed and stable for the life of the loan.

Bank loans typically are not.

Consult a financial advisor. Take the time to compare loan products offered by different banks to better ensure that you get the right loan product to hit your goal.

Types of Bank Loans

The standard mortgage is offered for the purpose of buying a home. Some of these programs are used to refinance a primary residence, vacation home, or for a one-to-four-unit investment property. The mortgage rate is usually fixed, locked in for the entire term of the loan.

Some mortgage products have a regimented adjustable-rate feature. To maintain their supply of funds to lend, mortgage companies sell the right to the income stream on these mortgages to quasi-government enterprises Fannie Mae and Freddie Mac. As long as the mortgage company has adhered to Fannie Mae and Freddie Mac guidelines and restrictions concerning the property, it can sell the rights to Fannie Mae and Freddie Mac for fresh funds to lend to the next customer. These guidelines include loan-to-value, and the borrower's credit, income, and assets

The Home Equity Line of Credit (HELOC) is a revolving line of credit secured as a lien on the real estate property, which acts much like a credit card that you can access when you need it. The interest rates are variable with no safety caps, although some lenders may offer a fixed rate for a specified period. If there are closing costs at all, they are minimal. The borrower pays an annual fee for the use of the credit line and a prepayment penalty if the HELOC gets closed prematurely.

In the first few years of the loan, which the lender calls the draw period, the borrower may be permitted to make interest-only payments on the balance. Later, following the draw period, the borrower will be required to pay P&I.

Most banks will loan up to 80% loan-to-value or combined-loan-to-value, and sometimes up to 90% combined. The interest rate is usually higher and credit restrictions tighter if the bank lends on the higher limit.

Example of the combined-loan-to-value structure:

Value of the home	$300,000
Maximum 90% combined-loan-to-value ($300K × 90%)	$270,000
Existing first mortgage balance	$150,000
Max HELOC funds to lend on 90% CLTV ($270K-$150K)	$120,000

The HELOC can also be used in combination with other loans to purchase a property. It can be used as a piggyback loan behind a purchase-money first mortgage. It can also be used as a "bridge loan" to provide down payment funds so the borrower's first mortgage does not require him to pay their private mortgage insurance.

Homebuyers use the piggyback combo and bridge loans when they need to purchase their new home before selling the old one.

They get a first mortgage through a mortgage company. Since the homebuyer does not have the proceeds from the sale of the old home yet, they use a HELOC second mortgage for the new home's down payment. Using the piggyback loan for down payment helps the borrower to secure a low enough mortgage balance to avoid having to pay the lender's private mortgage insurance. When the old home finally sells, the proceeds can be used to pay off the piggyback.

Sale price on new home	$400,000
New first mortgage	$320,000
New piggy-back second mortgage	$ 40,000
Down payment from buyer's funds	$ 40,000

If the existing home sells for $150,000 paying off the remaining mortgage balance of $100,000, profits would be plenty enough to pay off the $40,000 piggyback loan ... should the borrower choose to use the funds for that purpose.

Without a piggyback loan, the buyer would have to pay for private mortgage insurance to benefit the lender because the loan amount would have exceeded 80% loan-to-value.

Compare the cost using the piggyback second mortgage on the *new* home with using an Equity Line of Credit on the *old* home.

Sometimes the price on the new mortgage is much lower if there is not a piggyback in use. It may be a better deal to get a HELOC on the old house for $40,000, instead. Even if you pay more closing costs to the bank to get the HELOC on the old house, it still may turn out much better than paying points or a higher rate on your new first mortgage.

Samir Sader and his wife Sabba

Smooth Transition with a Combo Loan

Samir Sader and his wife, Sabba, sat at the kitchen table of the house they had called home for many years.

"We have made so many memories here. We're going to miss this place," Sabba sighed as she gazed around the kitchen and into the family room.

"The hard part will be packing up and moving fifteen years of our stuff to the new house," Samir added.

Samir and Sabba had finally found a home that would give them rest from the busy city and the noise. They had been visiting with a builder who called to let them know that he had a ready-made house with everything on their wish list.

Their first buyer was supposed to close in the next two weeks but backed out due to a family emergency.

If Samir and Sabba wanted the house, they would need to buy it right away or the builder would have to take the next offer.

Samir and Sabba had originally planned to sell their old home first because they did not owe much on the house and would realize a net profit of about $100,000. With those profits, they could easily pay down the purchase price of a new, more expensive home, to easily afford the mortgage payment without disturbing their retirement money.

How could they close on the new home right away before having a chance to sell the old home?

The Saders' mortgage officer connected them with a banker who agreed to give them an equity line of credit for $100,000 secured on their old home. They could use the proceeds from the equity line of credit to make the large down payment they wanted for the new home.

Samir and Sabba agreed to buy the new home from the builder and close in two weeks. The appraisal on the Saders' old home came in at $200,000. The balance on the existing first mortgage was a little over $75,000.

The maximum the bank could loan them on a second mortgage HELOC for the old home was 90% of the total value ... minus the first mortgage balance. That would mean $180,000 minus $75,000, which comes to $105,000.

This would give the Saders the $100,000 they needed to put down on the new home. The bank said they could get the money to the Saders in a week and a half.

"The best things in life are unexpected," Sabba said, smiling at the closing table.

"The best thing about *this* home purchase is that we won't have to rush to move all our things in one day," Samir added as he scribbled his signature on the last home closing document.

For Samir and Sabba, the equity line of credit was the key puzzle piece that made a quick buy possible. With a piggyback second mortgage on the new home, the rate on the new mortgage would have been more expensive because of the combined first mortgage and the piggyback loan. The price was better using the HELOC. The equity line of credit on the old home would be paid off as soon as their house sold, leaving the Saders with just the one low-balance mortgage and affordable monthly payment.

The Saders' combo loan transaction:

The Saders' old home value:	$200,000
The old home mortgage balance:	$ 75,000
The old home NEW Home Equity Line of Credit	$105,000
The Saders' new home purchase price:	$300,000
The HELOC on the old home used for down payment:	$105,000
New purchase first mortgage	$195,000

The HELOC is popular for combo transactions like the Saders' home purchase, as well as for covering family emergencies, buying a car, and more. Another popular Home Equity Loan has a fixed rate and works like a second mortgage. There are not as many flexible ways to use this program as there are for the HELOC.

The Construction Loan is used to provide funding for building a new home. Whether the borrower already owns or is buying the land, the construction loan can cover the cost to purchase and prepare the land, and to pay for the house plans and construction.

Once the home construction is complete, the borrower will need a permanent mortgage approved and ready to pay off the construction lender.

The borrower pays interest-only on the construction loan. The bank sets up a schedule of payments that coincide with the progressive stages of construction. The first draw on funds is taken to purchase the land and prepare for building. The second draw usually occurs after the foundation has been laid and the rough framing done. There are usually about six draws from start to finish on building a home.

The borrower only pays interest on the portion of the loan that has been issued. In the first part of the construction phase, the interest-only payment is small. As construction progresses and more money is issued to pay the builder, the borrower is paying interest-only on the larger loan amount.

In the meantime, the borrower needs to stay in touch with the mortgage company who will be the source for paying off the construction loan when the home is completed. As the time of completion gets closer, the borrower needs to send updated credit information, income, and asset documents and get the loan rate locked for permanent financing. Once the house is complete, the borrower uses the permanent mortgage loan to pay off the temporary construction loan.

To avoid problems with getting the construction loan approved, do not allow any work to begin on the construction site. The bank must issue a "no-start letter" proving no work has commenced and no materials have delivered onsite to ensure that the lender has priority over any potential lien claims of contractors. (This is specific to Tennessee law.)

The work will need to pass code inspections and stay within zoning restrictions. Modifications to the construction, increasing the costs, or affecting the value of the home must be cleared by the construction lender *and* the mortgage company.

Some mortgage companies offer a One-Time-Close Construction to Permanent Loan, which streamlines the process of working first with a construction lender and then with a mortgage company. Using the one-time close program, the mortgage company approves the borrow for the permanent loan and administers the period draws and inspections in-house, without using the bank.

Once the permanent loan is closed, the construction draws begin until all funds are issued to pay the builder and other costs. As construction is underway, it is not necessary to update documents to maintain the preapproval of the one-time close loan because the loan is already closed and the proceeds are being issued on a draw just like the construction loan lender would do at the bank.

The bridge loan works like the combo transaction with the mortgage and credit line. There are a number of different bridge loans, but most all of them provide the down payment and costs of purchasing a new home before the old home is able to sell.

The blanket loan is a bank loan that has multiple other properties to secure it. The terms on blanket loans can vary greatly from bank to bank. The borrower may not be able to get his loan approved unless the bank attaches additional assets as security.

The blanket mortgage is often used when a real estate investor is simultaneously purchasing four or five properties from one seller. The bank may give the investor one loan, but secure that loan on all of the properties in the transaction. Traditional mortgage companies do not issue blanket mortgages but banks have the flexibility to use them.

A disadvantage occurs when the borrower wants to sell or refinance a property under the blanket mortgage. Depending on the original loan terms, the borrower may have a problem getting one of the properties released from the security on the loan.

The hard money loan can come from banks, private lenders, or other places where someone is willing to lend their own money on agreed-upon terms. If the hard money loan is secured on real estate, it is important to check with a real estate attorney on the guidelines under the Secure and Fair Enforcement for Mortgage Licensing Act (S.A.F.E. Act).

Resources

https://singlefamily.fanniemae.com/originating-underwriting/
mortgage-products/construction-products Fannie Mae's guidelines on
construction loans

http://www.freddiemac.com/singlefamily/factsheets/sell/pdf/construction_
conversion_mortgage_637.pdf Freddie Mac's guidelines on construction
loans

CHAPTER 15

Credit

To contract new debts is not the way to pay old ones.
Attributed to President George Washington

Jump-Starting Your Credit Scores

JUST AS WE all have unique fingerprints, most adults have three credit scores. There are three major credit bureaus, each one providing a credit score for people with a credit history. The name of the game is to keep your credit scores as high as possible. The higher your score, the less you pay in borrowing costs when applying for credit.

Credit Score Rankings

- 780-850 **Top** credit scores
- 740 to 779 Really good scores that get you great rates and loan terms
- 700-739 Still good but not considered the best
- 660-699 Average

Once your scores dip below 660, you pay higher interest on loans and your payments are high.

Many mortgage companies across the country have minimum credit score limits—commonly 620 to 640.

Playing to win:

1. Check your credit through www.annualcreditreport.com or sign up for a credit monitoring service to keep tabs on your credit. Review reports to identify errors. Make corrections to the errors immediately.

2. Make your payments on time, never going over 30 days late. Payment history makes up about 35% of your score. If you get a 30-day late report on your credit from a creditor, your scores could fall 25 to 60 points or more.

3. Keep any revolving accounts such as credit cards UNDER 30% usage. Get your usage to 10% or lower, and you could raise your score dramatically in a short time. Credit usage makes up about 30% of your credit score.

   Example:
   Credit Card Credit Limit: $10,000
   Maximum usage: $3,000
   30% usage on a $10,000 credit line means the balance owed is never to exceed $3,000 at any time during the month.

4. Avoid "12 Months Same as Cash" accounts. These tend to score like a maxed-out credit card and can drop your scores 60 to 100 points quickly.

5. Old, established credit card history results in better scores. Length of time on a credit account makes up about 15% of your score. An account older than six months helps you a little. An account five years and older helps you a lot. Don't close credit card accounts unless they have a high annual fee.

6. Credit inquiries and getting new credit makes up about 10% of your score. Be careful about accumulating inquiries on your report because these can have a negative impact. When shopping for a mortgage—that is, when only other mortgage companies pull your credit within a 14- to 45-day period—the inquiries appear but should not penalize you so that you can shop without it hurting your rating.

7. Some clients have asked, "Why do I even *need* to pay off this collection balance?" The reason we pay off collections is that it is the right thing to do. If you receive notice of a creditor about to file against you, immediately contact them and pay the bill, or set up amicable payment terms. Collections stay on your account for seven

years. Even if you pay it off, it remains on your credit report as "not paid as agreed."

As you prepare for a mortgage application, check with your lender before paying off a collection. When you pay it, the creditor reports you "paid." Most see this as a good thing. Human underwriters seem to look favorably when they see that the borrower has paid the bill. However, the credit scoring machine sees it as another derogatory report because a numerical code for the "collection tradeline" is updated in the system.

Talk with your lender.

Depending on the amount owed and the cumulative amounts owed on multiple collections, the mortgage underwriting may require you to pay them off, anyway; but, if the collection accounts are old, they might not have a great impact on your scores at the moment the credit bureau pulls the report. Check with your lender before taking action if you are about to make a major purchase.

8. Pay off debt rather than moving it around. A big influence on your score is how you handle revolving credit accounts. Be sure to make your mortgage and car payments on time, but revolving account usage is a big factor in determining your credit score, too.

9. Don't open multiple new credit cards that you don't need just to increase your available credit. This method could lower your score.

10. If you are newly building credit, don't open a lot of new accounts quickly. New accounts lower your average "account age," which will have a negative effect on your score. Opening many new accounts in a short time can make you look risky to a lender.

11. Don't agree to cosign with anyone. If the borrower quits paying, you are responsible. If the borrower is over 30 days late with payments, this negative reporting is reflected on *your* credit report, too.

12. Don't open any new accounts or make a purchase on credit while applying for a mortgage. Just wait until *after* you close on the home.

13. Try to avoid bankruptcy if you can feasibly pay your accounts in a reasonable amount of time. Bankruptcies, home foreclosures, and short sales are bad for your credit score and reflect poorly on you as a borrower.

14. What does someone do who has NO credit? They will be limited on available mortgage products as these loans will have to be manually underwritten under the strictest guidelines. Most often, these

products require the borrower to document three or four seasoned non-traditional credit accounts like paid utility bills, telephone service, rent, or insurance payments. If you show any derogatory marks on your report, you will be ineligible to use non-traditional credit methods in lieu of credit history.

Most lenders will refer to something called the FICO score to determine your eligibility for a loan. The Consumer Financial Protection Bureau (CFPB) at consumerfinance.gov defines FICO this way:

FICO stands for the Fair Isaac Corporation. FICO was a pioneer in developing a method for calculating credit scores based on information collected by credit reporting agencies. Today, other companies also have credit scoring formulas ("models"), but most lenders still use FICO scores when deciding whether to offer you a loan or credit card, and in setting the rate and terms. Banks may also use FICO scores when approving checking and savings account applications and setting the terms of those accounts. —CFPB, "What is a FICO score?"[2]

Myths About What Affects Your FICO Score

1. **Myth # 1:** You have to carry a debt balance to create a score.
   Truth: You need some credit history over the last two years, but you do NOT have to carry a balance on a credit card in order to obtain a high score.

2. **Myth # 2:** Your income affects your score.
   Truth: Your income does NOT affect your score.

3. **Myth # 3:** You and your spouse share a credit score.
   Truth: You and your spouse do NOT share a credit score. You each develop your own unique scores based on your individual activity.

4. **Myth # 4:** Closing all my accounts is a good thing.

---

[2] https://www.consumerfinance.gov/ask-cfpb/what-is-a-fico-score-en-1883/

Truth: Closing all your accounts is NOT a good thing. Keeping the credit card accounts open and in good standing is a good thing, especially if the accounts are older.

(Disclaimer: The algorithms for credit score calculation can change over time. Periodically check websites like **www.myfico.com** and the credit bureau websites for updates.)

The Big Three Credit Bureaus and How to Contact Them

Take Your Own Credit Temperature

To set out on a road to good credit, first know what your credit looks like today.

Every year you are allowed to check your own credit for free by going to **www.annualcreditreport.com.** Check all three credit bureaus to make sure there are no errors on your report.

If you find errors, compose a letter to contact all three bureaus and the merchant reporting the erroneous credit. In the letter, make sure you identify yourself, your social security number (to the bureaus), and your address and contact information. Inform them of the error and ask for the erroneous credit to be removed. Be sure and include the merchant's name, address, phone number, and account number. The merchant reporting erroneous credit has a limited time to respond to your request, so it is a good idea to get cracking on the mailed letter. You should hear back in about 30 to 60 days.

Do-It-Yourself Credit Fix

If some of the negative credit reporting was not in error but really was bad credit on your part, there may be some actions you can take to lessen the negative blow.

If you have collection accounts showing balances still owing, call the creditor. Ask them to agree to periodically pause reporting on that collection account. They may be willing to negotiate with you.

Each time a late payment or collection account gets reported on your credit, it is like a sucker punch to the gut for your credit scores. Even when you set up a payment plan in exchange for a pause on negative reports, the negative mark stays and does not leave for seven years from the last negative report.

Check with the credit bureau or a licensed credit counselor. If the collection agency does not have your social security number on file, they may not have any debt instruments signed by you either. Do not give them your full social security number. Only give the last 4 digits of social for identification. If they have no record that you owe them, you may consider writing them a registered letter asking them to remove any derogatory reports regarding the collection account.

Equifax Information Services
www.equifax.com
PO BOX 740241
Atlanta, GA 30374-0241
(800) 685-1111

Experian
www.experian.com/reportaccess
701 Experian Parkway
PO BOX 2002
Allen, TX 75013
(888) 397-3742

Transunion Consumer Relations
www.transunion.com/myoptions
2 Baldwin Place
PO BOX 1000
Chester, PA 19022
(800) 888-4213

The Tale of Two Borrowers
(Stories as Told on the Radio Show "Real Estate Mortgage Shoppe")

Tale #1: Terrance and Tamika Thomas lived a fairly comfortable life, steadily working at their careers, supporting their almost-grown children, and living in the same house they had owned for over ten years. Their lives were about to change. Their oldest child was graduating college that year and their youngest would be graduating and leaving home the following. Terrance and Tamika wanted to move out to the country. For years, Terrance dreamed of having his own workshop to fix stuff and make some money doing his hobby.

Tamika's dream was to have a covered back patio with a fancy barbecue grill and a backyard view of the woods. She had been eyeing those open kitchen plans with the most up-to-date appliances, complete with double oven. The house they wanted had all of this and more.

Even though Terrance and Tamika's life was going well and they seemed to effortlessly have whatever they needed, that is not how their marriage started many years before.

Several years earlier, life for the Thomases could be described as a tire running off the road, a train jumping off the track, and an accident waiting to happen.

Tamika's impulse-buying on credit, and Terrance's lack of discipline with paying bills and saving money caused heartache and disappointment. The financial stress almost cost them their marriage.

About three years after taking their wedding vows, Terrance and Tamika got into a financial freedom class through their church. It was a well-known national program to get families out of debt. They committed, and with encouragement from friends and family, the Thomases emerged from the debt-free program with some savings in the bank, a paid-off house, and very high credit scores.

Terrance and Tamika found a house in the country that they really liked. It was not everything they wanted. The house was lacking a covered back patio, and the workshop was not completely finished … but the price was right. Their expert realtor referred them to an expert mortgage lender.

Since Terrance and Tamika's credit was so good and they had saved extra money to put down on the new house, they enjoyed the lowest mortgage rate and an even lower monthly payment. It would not take them long to gradually pay off this house. The Thomas family had such good credit and buying power that their mortgage and homebuying process could only be described as "Easy Peasy."

Tale #2: Sam and Sally Smith were newly married and expecting their first  child. Saddled with student loan debt, they were strapped for cash and existing in an apartment too small for their expanding family. Sam regretted his carefree days in college charging up the credit cards he accepted in the mail. It was so easy to use them, but a few missed payments and a collection account tanked his scores.

When Sam was denied credit to purchase a car he needed to commute to work, reality hit like a slap in the face. It was time to make and stick to a plan until his credit started working *for* him instead of against him.

Sally's story was different. She had stayed away from credit altogether and simply had no credit score. Her income was too low to qualify for a house on her own, so the plan was to build her credit and make Sam's credit better.

In the meantime, Sam had to buy a cheap car he described as a "rust bucket on a roller skate." He paid way over blue book value using a loan with a double-digit interest rate. He described the payment as: "Ouch!"

When Sam and Sally applied for a mortgage to get out of the cramped apartment and into a house, the news was not what they wanted to hear. Even if he could improve his credit score up to 640 from his current 565 score, he would pay about a half-point higher on the interest rate. Over a period of time, the financing would cost him almost $10,000 more than if his scores were higher ... but Sam had a plan to move the dial up in just a few months, and Sally's plan could get her to a decent score in only 30 days.

The Tale Continues...

Terrance and Tamika bought their country house with a workshop and began gradually making it into the dream home they envisioned.

About a month after moving in, they invited family and church friends for dinner and house warming. Walking through the door with a bag of chips and a container of homemade salsa ... were Sammy and Sally Smith.

During the course of the evening festivities, Sammy and Sally shared with Terrance and Tamika their personal dream of owning a home. They shared their disappointing experience of being turned down for a home loan due to credit snafus.

Terrance and Tamika confessed to their own past history of credit skids and smashes. They shared how their choice to get help and get disciplined in their finances during earlier years set them free to leave peacefully and joyfully with their children now. Terrance connected the Smiths with the mortgage officer who had helped them many years before, and Sammy and Sally were well on their way to fulfilling the dream of owning their own home.

Epilogue

Terrance and Tamika are living happily in their new home in the country. Sammy has been helping Terrance finish out the workshop, building benches and racks and things. Tamika and Sally have been painting and staining the cabinets in the kitchen, lightening up the space to make it feel even more open and inviting.

Sammy set up a payment plan to deal with past due credit cards that had been haunting him. He made a deal with the card companies not to report negatively on him so long as he made regular, timely payments to finish the debts.

He went online and signed up for a well-known secured credit card. This type of card required him to send the credit card company $300 of his own money. He then borrowed against the account, keeping a balance of no more than $25/month for three months. This resulted in an extra 50 points on his credit score.

Sally's parents added her to one of their seasoned, low usage credit cards which just about instantly popped her credit score up from zero to around 680.

Sammy and Sally are working with the same realtor who helped Terrance and Tamika. They know what they want in a house, including a special room for their new baby. They are willing to start small so they can stay on a less stressful budget and enjoy life a lot more.

The Flannerys

From Heavy Hardships to Homeownership

One young family, the Flannerys, lost their jobs, their cars, and their home during the economic downturn around 2010. They had two young children and yearned to own their own home again so their children could play outside safely and not be cooped up in an apartment.

The loss of their car plus health issues delayed this couple getting the better-paying jobs they needed, making the cycle of hardship press down on them even more. Mr. Flannery said, "Time after time I would finally get up on my feet when something else would crash in and take me down again. It was like a terrible movie where you just want to click off the television, but you can't because the movie is about *you* and *you* are the actor on the stage and the film is still rolling."

The Flannerys considered signing up for a program to help them resolve some debt issues, but there was a cost to the program. They tried something else, but it didn't work, either. They found no quick fixes. One evening at church, they went to a special meeting about managing finances, and that is when I got to meet the Flannerys.

Through a strong faith in God and tenacious effort to work within their budget, applying extra cash to paying off debt and paying down credit cards, the Flannerys emerged debt-free a few years later. I got to be on their homebuying journey as their lender. The day of the loan closing was a spectacular celebration for the Flannerys ... and me.

Phillip and Farrah Fenton

Ratcheting up the Credit Score to Ratchet Down the Price

Phillip and Farrah Fenton had been married over a year and were expecting their first child. As newlyweds, they didn't mind living cramped in a tiny house in a family member's backyard ... but now they had the baby to think about.

Phillip's credit score was suffering because of bills he had not paid and others he had racked up from his carefree college days.

In order to put himself and his family into a better position, Phillip and I talked strategy. With the help of his wife, he disciplined himself to aggressively pay down the balances on revolving credit card accounts, and to keep the owed balances under 30% usage. His credit score started improving.

After adding several points to his credit score, Phillip was in a position to get a lot lower mortgage interest rate. As bragging rights for the Fentons—they locked in a lower rate than they ever thought possible ... leaving them with more money to spend on the baby.

Resources

The site www.MyFico.com shows you where to concentrate on getting the best and quickest results to jumpstart excellent credit scores. You can also find help by contacting the credit bureaus.

The Fair Credit and Reporting Act (FCRA) https://www.consumerfinance. gov/compliance/compliance-resources/other-applicable-requirements/ fair-credit-reporting-act/

The Fair Debt Collection Practices Act (FDCPA) https://www.consumerfinance. gov/about-us/newsroom/consumer-financial-protection-bureau-issues-final- rule-implement-fair-debt-collection-practices-act/

The Fair Credit Billing Act (FCBA) https://www.ftc.gov/enforcement/statutes/fair-credit-billing-act

The Fair and Accurate Credit Transactions Act of 2003 (FACTA) https://www.ftc.gov/enforcement/statutes/fair-accurate-credit-transactions-act-2003

Credit Card Accountability, Responsibility and Disclosure Act (CARD ACT) https://www.ftc.gov/enforcement/statutes/credit-card-accountability-responsibility-and-disclosure-act-2009-credit-card

CHAPTER 16

Overcoming Income Barriers to Loan Approval

"A really good CPA makes it tough for a mortgage loan officer to qualify their customer."

Anonymous

MORE THAN BOOKS and classes, experience has been a great teacher when it comes to the twisting, winding path that a borrower's income can take.

Each bend in the road can change the way a mortgage underwriter calculates the qualifying income amount. Getting the borrower's income documents up front can bring peace of mind and save everyone negative surprises.

Lenders consider income one of the pillars of loan approval. Not only do you have to verify the amount of your income, but also the stability of that income. If the borrower can document that the income is likely to continue for the next 36 months, usually the lender will use it.

If a marital dissolution agreement says that the borrower gets $600 per month until the child turns 18, but the child is already 15 years old, there is less than 36 months left on the agreement and this income cannot be used. If the child is only 14 years old but the $600 per month income is sporadic and not paid as agreed, the income is not considered stable and cannot be used.

Divorce agreements can be tricky.

I have seen mortgage clients negotiate to get child support and alimony income for a full five years or more in order to keep that stable, qualified income for more than enough time to find the house they want.

A salary or regular hourly income is considered most stable when it is from an employer that withholds the taxes and other deductions on W-2 income. Having less than two years' job history can be problematic. One way to demonstrate job stability is to show that you have been in the same *line* of work or in school for that line of work for at least two years. Lenders do not factor income from temporary employees. When the borrower can show that he is a permanent employee, the income is considered stable again.

Two consecutive years of income history are required for someone working as a subcontractor who files a 1099 form. Two years are required for the borrower who is self-employed or who owns 25% or more of a company. Lenders do make exceptions with the right documentation to allow a shorter history of self-employment, but generally, a two-year minimum history of self-employment income is required.

While in the middle of the loan process, avoid switching from a guaranteed W-2 income to a subcontractor 1099 income. The 1099 sub-contractor income will require a one- or two-year history.

Example: Albert Abbott was fresh out of the military with a new job. The salary wasn't great but at least he could qualify for a mortgage to buy the house he wanted.

As our mortgage team was processing Albert's papers, we noticed that, in the middle of the loan process, Albert had switched from being a salaried employee to a 1099 subcontractor position.

As a 1099 worker, the employer no longer withheld federal taxes and Albert was considered self-employed as a subcontractor.

When I asked Albert about the switch from employee to self-employed, he answered, "Because I can make a lot more money."

His eyes bulged when I informed him that the government mortgage program he wanted would not allow us to count any of his self-employment income until he had two or more years' track record on the same job.

Albert decided that "less is more" and arranged with his employer to return him to employee status, even if he was making less money. At least he would be able to qualify for his mortgage.

Some mortgage clients who have been self-employed for two or more years still have problems getting qualified because they don't show enough income on the front page of their tax return. An experienced lender can go into the back pages of the tax return to look for certain expenses that can be added back to the income column, creating more qualified income for the borrower.

Adding Income

If the borrower has been working multiple jobs simultaneously for the last two consecutive years, there is a history of the income and the borrower's ability to work multiple jobs. It is possible the lender can use the secondary income since it is stable and continuous.

Some of the affordable conventional loan products allow the borrower to use boarder income if she can prove that she has received income from this boarder for at least the last twelve consecutive months and the boarder will continue to pay rent.

Retirement and social security income can be "grossed up" by about 25% when the income is not taxed. Sometimes adding 25% to the actual retirement income can be the difference between an approval or denial.

Income from rental properties, royalties, inheritance, annuity, and other sources might be used to qualify the borrower if the income is stable and properly documented.

Cosigners are sometimes needed to help a borrower qualify for a mortgage. The cosigner would need to have good credit, adequate income, and not a lot of debt obligations. Adding the cosigner is many times the answer to getting loan approval.

Self-employment income can be improved if the lender finds expenses considered "paper losses" that can be added back to total income. Such paper losses include depreciation on equipment, business use of the home, and commuting expenses up to about 25 cents per depreciable business mile. Once-in-a-lifetime expenses can be added back to income if properly documented. If the borrower has been self-employed in this business for over five years, the underwriting software will sometimes only require income to be calculated from the most recent tax return instead of requiring an average of two tax years.

Mr. Palmer

Business Owner Overcomes

This story illustrates some barriers that self-employed borrowers may smack into when applying for a mortgage loan.

Mr. Patrick Palmer had invested and worked long and hard in his own successful business for over 10 years. For the last several months, he struggled with fatigue and burnout. What Mr. Palmer needed was a change of scenery—like a nicer house with a view in the country.

On the day Mr. Palmer saw his dream home for sale, he made an offer to the seller. For the first time in months, he felt an exhilarating rush of hope that moving into this home with its serene outdoor space would provide the relief he needed from living so close to his business.

Mr. Palmer confidently marched into his bank to get his mortgage approved. He was shocked when the banker shook his head and handed him back his tax returns.

The next stop was to the realtor's preferred lender. Again, the answer was no. Too little income showed on his tax returns.

A friend referred Mr. Palmer to me.

We scanned over his last two years' tax returns, and in just a few minutes I had his preapproval letter ready to go. "How did you *do* that?" he happily demanded.

I explained to Mr. Palmer that instead of starting at the front of his tax returns, I started at the back. Then, I located expenses we could legally add back into his income as those tax write-offs were paper losses only.

These paper losses included depreciation on equipment, business use of the residence, and the depreciable part of business mileage. Other expenses that can sometimes work with the right documentation include once-in-a-life-time expenses. Calculating self-employment income from tax returns requires attention to detail. We found enough of these paper losses to boost his qualified income. Mr. Palmer was approved and bought his dream home!

Restructuring Debt to Improve Debt-to-Income Ratio

We've explored methods of increasing income to qualify for a mortgage. The other side of the seesaw is reducing debt to get the debt-to-income ratio in line.

Debt can be reduced or eliminated by paying it down, paying it off, restructuring the debt so the payment is not as high, or getting someone else to take the payment out of the borrower's name and into his own.

Other people's debt is a great place to start looking for methods of reducing debt. Check for accounts that are paid by someone else other than the borrower. This could be a credit card that the borrower is only authorized to use, but in a different person's name. This could be a student loan or car that the borrower cosigned for someone else, and which can be verified paid as agreed by that person (not the borrower) for the last 12 consecutive months.

Another overlooked strategy is for a family member to assume a borrower's debt into their own name, such as a car payment. It would be especially helpful if the family member was also driving the car or using the product.

Consolidating and restructuring debt to create a much lower payment can help the borrower's overall debt-to-income ratio. Mortgage clients motivated to get their mortgage approved: try refinancing a car loan from $500 per month down to a $300 per month payment. Consolidate student loans. Most loan products count one percent of the unpaid student loans as the qualifying debt payment. The right mortgage product will have ways to reduce the student loan qualifying payment to help them get approved.

CHAPTER 17

Overcoming Barriers Due to Lack of Assets

Remember, the treasure doesn't do the hunting.

Anonymous

"Show Me the Money": Treasure Hunting for Closing Funds

JERRY MCGUIRE WAS a 1996 award winning film with the renowned catch phrase, "Show me the money!" Lenders have been repeating this to their borrowers for years. Where can borrowers go to find money when they do not have it to show?

Three areas to search are the borrower's forgotten assets, gifts from family or employers, and move-in costs paid by third parties. Sinking a shovel into these three areas has turned up pay dirt for many. Here is a treasure hunting map detailing some clues.

Gifts: Gifts can come from family members or employers. The permitted amount of the donation varies according to different loan programs. The donor is required to document their source of funds when the money is a gift not requiring repayment. If the donor does not want to liquidate an asset such as a stock fund, he can borrow against the asset to give to the donee.

Borrower's Forgotten Assets: Many times, the borrower does not realize the insurance she purchased years ago has a cash value that can be borrowed to pay move-in costs. Whole life insurance policies or annuities may have a cash value that can be loaned.

So long as the borrower is the owner, certificates of deposit, stocks and bonds, and durable assets such as cars can be acceptable for securing a loan to fund the closing. The debt must be added into the debt-to-income ratios for qualifying purposes.

Tax Refunds can provide a surprising source of closing funds.

IRAs, 401(k)s, and Retirement Funds are also options, but there can be heavy financial penalties for pulling money from some of these sources. Some companies do allow the homebuyer to borrow against these assets with no penalty. The repayment terms may be calculated in the borrower's debt-to-income ratio. In some cases, the borrower does not have to immediately reimburse the 401(k). Check with your 401(k) administrator.

Sale or Cash-Out Refinance of a currently owned property can generate needed funds to close on a new one. Lenders will require the official Closing Disclosure proving the source of funds.

Most loan programs do not allow closing funds to come from an unsecured loan. If the money to close is borrowed, it must be secured on something with adequate, verified value.

Move-in Costs Paid by Third Parties: Sellers are as motivated to sell a house as the buyer is to purchase. Sellers can pay up to 6% of the sale price toward the buyer's costs on FHA loans. If the borrower is getting a conventional loan above 90% loan-to-value the seller can pay 3%. If the loan-to-value is 90% or less, the seller is allowed to pay costs up to 6% of the sale price or value, whichever is less.

Investor loans allow the sellers to pay no more than 2% towards buyer costs.

Lenders are also motivated to close the transaction. To cover the borrower's prepaid taxes and insurance or some of the closing costs, they can slightly bump up the interest rate and call it "premium pricing." In most cases the rate is increased .25% and the difference in the monthly payment is minimal.

Charitable organizations and government agencies such as Tennessee Housing Development Agency have programs that provide down payment assistance to borrowers. Some of the well- known programs are City of Memphis Down Payment Assistance, Shelby County Down Payment Assistance, and United Housing, Inc. For down payment assistance programs in other cities and states, check with Rob Chrane at Down Payment Resource, supported by Housing Finance Agencies across the country. Search for assistance programs in YOUR city and state: **http:// downpaymentresource.com/about/leadership/**

For down payment assistance grants and loans, borrowers are required to meet a minimum or maximum annual income guideline and sometimes are required to be first-time homebuyers. First-time homebuyers are defined as buyers who have not owned real estate in the last two to three years. There are exceptions to the first-time homebuyer rules.

The Johanssons

A Triumphant Ending

You could say we are beginning this story at the end—the end of the home buying and mortgage process that culminates at the real estate closing table. I got to attend the closing with two of my mortgage clients—a married couple who have spent much of their lives serving others overseas. On returning stateside they really wanted to own their first home. Their challenge was lacking the funds to close and a large enough income to afford the payment on a house like the one they needed.

The Johanssons put a good realtor on their team, who listened to their needs and wants. For months, their realtor watched the market daily until she found a home that the Johanssons knew was meant to be theirs.

The Johanssons laid out their limits on payments and move-in costs. To cover the price of the house with a normal down payment would wreck their budget and leave them no emergency funds.

However, because of their income level and the home's location, they qualified for a special down payment assistance product that offered over $10,000 in down payment assistance and a lower-than-market interest rate.

Using this product, the house was well within their grasp. The payment was comfortable and they had emergency funds left over.

When we all arrived at the title office to complete the closing of the loan and transfer of title to the Johanssons, it was celebration time. While Mr. Johansson signed the papers, Mrs. Johansson talked excitedly about how she planned to decorate the home and make it a happy place for their family and friends to come visit. When the last paper was signed and notarized, Mr. and Mrs. Johansson rushed into each other's arms in celebration of achieving their dream of owning a home. We were all laughing and cheering. It was a long-won victory.

As we took pictures and shared more stories of the Johanssons' journey to homeownership, I felt that rush of happiness and fulfillment, knowing I played a role in making a lifelong dream come true for this very deserving couple. I reminded myself, "This is why I get up, get ready, and get to work each day. This is why I do what I do as a mortgage loan officer."

Resources

http://downpaymentresource.com/about/leadership/ The Down Payment
Resource Center

CHAPTER 18

Overcoming Appraisal Challenges

What Is the Purpose of a Real Estate Appraisal?

DUE TO STRICT rules prohibiting mortgage loan officers from talking with appraisers on a shared case, appraisers can seem to be illusive and mysterious in their ways. As the radio talk show host on Real Estate Mortgage Shoppe, I have gained a wealth of knowledge about appraisals from my appraiser co-hosts and guests. Over the course of several years, these professionals have taught me and our radio listeners great ways to solve challenges connected to your home appraisal.

Lenders almost always get a licensed appraiser to give an unbiased opinion of a home's value when the home is being used as collateral for the loan. Depending on the particular loan product, appraisers may have strong limitations and parameters on what they can consider "comparable sales"—commonly called "comps"—to help determine value. Therefore, the value on an appraisal for, say, an FHA and a conventional loan may differ.

Under the Dodd-Frank Act, mortgage companies are required to order appraisals through an approved Appraisal Management Company (AMC). This "firewall" was put in place to prevent collusion between mortgage companies and appraisers. That means that if you are a borrower buying or refinancing a home, the mortgage company cannot use your chosen appraiser and they cannot use an appraisal that you ordered yourself. The AMC—not the mortgage company—selects the appraiser. There are some exceptions to this rule.

Appraisers use a method called "bracketing" to select the comps that are similar to the home being appraised in the same general area. One comp reflects a home with higher value and another will reflect a lower value. When the appraiser uses bracketing, they will examine recent sales of similar homes both *superior* and *inferior* to the home being appraised; for example, houses both bigger and smaller, newer and older.

Here are some factors that appraisers use when determining the value of a home:

- sale prices over the last six months or less of homes similar to the home being appraised and in the same general neighborhood
- square footage of the heated space and living area
- condition of the home compared to other homes in the area
- construction quality
- time homes in the area remain on the market before being sold
- price and value trends of homes selling in the neighborhood
- lot size compared to the home
- zoning restrictions
- convenience of the layout
- conformity to surrounding homes
- other amenities like a swimming pool

Appraisal Barriers to Overcome

1. The values of other homes in the neighborhood greatly affect the appraisal value. If the home is over-built with a significant amount of square footage more than that of surrounding homes, the appraisal may not come in as high as expected. In this case, rearrange the financing goal to work with a lower appraisal value and lower loan amount. Sometimes that requires the borrower using a different property or asset they own to secure the needed financing.
2. If the home is a manufactured home, berm home, log home, or geodesic home, and it is the only home with that type of construction in the neighborhood, this could be problematic. Sometimes the appraiser will look for recent sales of similar construction in neighborhoods further from the subject property. The mortgage lenders usually require that the appraiser show one or two other

comparable properties with the same construction type that have sold within the last twelve months.

3. Sometimes the appraiser finds two separate houses sitting on the same parcel number. To provide fair comps, the appraiser must show another subject property with two homes on the same parcel that have sold in the last twelve months, but this can be rare and difficult to find. To solve this problem, if the second home is small enough, simply removing the kitchen stove can qualify the second property to be valued as a workshop rather than a separate residential dwelling.

4. The condition of the home can create obstacles to getting the value needed, or getting approval from the mortgage company's underwriting department. Appraisers notate repairs that affect the *structure, security and sanitation* of the home. Mortgage companies require these types of repairs to be completed before closing.

Repairs that affect the structure include rotted wood; foundation problems; roof leaks or missing shingles; peeling paint (especially if the home was built prior to 1978); broken siding; electrical, plumbing, or heating problems; or issues with the air and duct systems.

Repairs affecting the security of the home include doors that do not operate correctly, broken locks, or open access to the home from outside.

Repairs pertaining to the sanitation of the home include drainage problems; faulty water supply and septic issues; mold; and more.

Most underwriters want the trouble areas corrected *before* closing, but there are some workarounds when items can be fixed after closing, too.

When the repairs must be fixed before closing, the buyer and seller negotiate who will pay for which repairs. If the buyer pays, the mortgage company will have to verify in the borrower's asset accounts that they have the funds to cover closing and repair costs. If the seller pays, then he or she cannot pay the buyer with a "repair allowance." Most traditional mortgage programs no longer allow repair allowances or "carpet and paint allowances."

In cases like this, the seller could put the money in escrow to be paid to the repair vendor after closing. Some loan programs require the seller to pay one-and-a-half times the amount of the contractor's bid into the repair escrow account. The extra fifty percent is simply a cushion to make sure, if the repair bill ended up higher than estimated, the seller would have the money to complete repairs. If unused, the extra fifty percent can be paid back to the seller when all the work is complete.

Should weather prevent the job's completion before closing, the mortgage underwriting guidelines permit certain repair items to be completed thereafter. These include landscaping and outdoor painting. In some locations, the mortgage company can permit the heating and air conditioning to be installed after closing to prevent them from being stolen before the new homeowners move into the property.

Disputing the Low Appraisal Value

Mortgage companies calculate the borrower's maximum loan amount based on the sale price or appraisal value, whichever is less. In a case where the purchase agreement is subject to an appraisal **at or above** asking price, most contracts will protect the home buyer.

In the case of an appraisal lower than asking, the seller can choose to lower the price; the buyer could choose to pay above-value; or both parties could walk away from the agreement.

When the seller cannot afford to drop the price on the home, or the transaction is a refinance that will only work with a higher appraised value, the parties to the transaction are motivated to look for ways to get the value higher.

Federal laws prohibit lenders from pressuring appraisers to increase the value on a home. However, the parties to the transaction can review the appraisal to look for errors in the data used to determine the value. If they find a potential error, the appraisal can be contested through the appraisal management company.

Here is how one realtor contested an appraisal for his sellers and buyers.

The sellers were motivated to close by the end of the month and the buyers were, too. The sellers had spent over $15,000 upgrading their home a few years prior to listing it for sale. It had the latest kitchen and bathroom fixtures, flooring and countertops. Other updated homes in the neighborhood had been selling for $285,000. The sellers wanted to sell quickly so they listed at $280,000. Randy the Realtor considered this an easy transaction—until the appraisal was completed.

The appraisal came back with a value of only $270,000. The sellers would be losing money if they sold their home for $270,000 and they told Randy the Realtor they would pull it off the market and rent it before selling at such a low price.

The buyers wanted the home and asked the realtor if he would review it to find out why the value came in so far below asking price. Randy was familiar with the homes in the surrounding area. After reviewing the appraisal, Randy the Realtor discovered that the comparable sales the appraiser used in determining value included two homes that had never been refurbished and updated.

The buyers, using information they got from Randy's research, composed a very respectful letter to the appraisal management company, pointing out the fact that the comps selected by the appraiser did not have the upgrades and updates that the sellers had invested into the subject home. With their dispute letter, they included some comparable sales that *did* have similar upgrades. These homes had sold for much higher than those used in the appraisal.

A few days following submission of the letter, the lender received notice that the new data had been reviewed and the value was increased by $8,000. It was less than the desired $10,000, but enough to make the numbers work for both buyers and sellers.

Martin and Maria Miller

Call on Resources to Get the Second Home They Need

Martin and Maria moved more than a thousand miles from the place where they had lived and built a life with their children. After the kids were older, the couple had an opportunity to take over a business on the other side of the country, and they took it. Later, their children got jobs in different areas of the country. The Martins yearned to have a central rallying place where their family could get together for the holidays and gatherings.

A close family friend from their hometown knew of their desire for a second home in the old neighborhood. This close friend set them up with a realtor who found them a house close to where they once lived. It was beaten up and needed a good cleaning, some carpentry, and a bit of new sheetrock.

Halfway through the loan process, the appraisal came in with a mile-long list of items that could affect the structure, safety, and sanitation on the house. Due to the types of repairs needed, the lender required these repairs to be completed BEFORE closing.

The Millers realized with a sinking feeling that they had just spent hundreds of dollars on an appraisal and now seemed to be in a catch-22. They could not close on the home until repairs were done, but the seller did not have the money for repairs until after the closing. In so many cases, this is where the bargain deal dies.

Nevertheless, good friends can be valuable, especially when their trade is fixing and building houses. Their hometown friend got the list of needed repairs and whistled up his construction buddies. Everyone agreed to work for just about free just to help the Millers.

They put together an itemized agreement to start work when the loan was approved for all but the repairs. The seller signed the agreement that he would pay the hometown friend and his pals on closing day when he got the funds. Once the loan was preapproved by the lender's underwriter, hometown friend and his pals went to work. The appraiser went back to the house to verify the completed repairs so the Millers could quickly close on their home, where they and the rest of their family could gather together in their former hometown ... all thanks to their good-hearted hometown friend ... whom they now looked forward to having over for their celebratory dinner!

Resources

https://www.nar.realtor/appraisal-valuation National Association of Realtors

CHAPTER 19

Mortgage Underwriting Software – Getting Loan Approval

If you think nobody cares if you are dead or alive, try missing a couple of mortgage payments.

Anonymous

WOULDN'T YOU AGREE that it is easier to win at a game when you know the rules? Once you know the rules, you can plan your offensive and defensive strategies to get to the goal faster. A mortgage originator's game plan takes him to the goal of getting loans approved quickly and with the least resistance.

Fannie Mae and Freddie Mac are the largest agencies that purchase mortgage loans from mortgage lenders. Fannie Mae and Freddie Mac issue their loan guidelines and provide underwriting software to help lenders determine the applicant's eligibility for a loan program. Once the borrower's information is entered, the underwriting software performs a risk-based analysis to assess whether a borrower's strengths in one area can offset risk factors in other areas.

Fannie Mae and Freddie Mac risk-based underwriting evaluates credit-related factors such as credit payment history, delinquent accounts, public records, and credit inquiries. Non-credit related factors are also evaluated and include:

- Equity and loan-to-value
- Liquid reserves
- Debt-to-income ratio

- Loan purpose
- Loan type
- Loan term
- Property type
- Number of borrowers
- Self-employed borrowers
- Occupancy

The most important factors are equity, credit history, and liquid reserves. Research conducted by Fannie Mae and Freddie Mac has demonstrated a lesser likelihood of loan default when the borrower has made a higher down payment, managed their finances well, and has a fair amount of money left in the bank after closing. For this reason, the borrower might *not* get a loan approval if she uses her savings to reduce her monthly bills instead of leaving savings in the bank. In many cases, it *is* better for the borrower to have a higher-than-normal debt-to-income ratio rather than using her funds to pay down excessive debts. *Money left in the bank after closing gives the borrower a much better advantage in the underwriting evaluation.*

Equity in the home or a large down payment lessens the risk to the lender unless the down payment was a gift from someone outside the transaction. Borrowers who put little of their own money into the transaction may still be approved, but they also could be considered too risky.

The underwriting systems consider the borrower's FICO score along with how long credit has been established, payment history, and public records. A borrower with a good credit history probably has a high FICO score (760 or above). An account that has been established for a long time is usually considered less risky than a newly established credit account.

Payment history has a significant impact on risk-based evaluation and can cause problems with getting a loan approval if the borrower has made payments over 30 days late within the last two years. If the delinquency is more recent, the loan is considered a higher risk.

Credit bureaus advise keeping credit card balances under 50% of the credit limit. Overextended credit indicates a riskier borrower. Points may be added to the credit score if the borrower shows a revolving credit under 30% of max. Public records such as bankruptcies, foreclosures, judgments, and liens indicate higher risk and remain on the credit report longer.

Total debt-to-income is the sum of the monthly house payment, existing car loans, credit card minimum payments, and the like, divided by gross monthly income. The highest suggested debt ratio for a borrower is 43% of gross income. However, the mortgage underwriting systems have been known to approve loans with debt-to-income ratios as high as 50% or more if other factors such as liquid assets or high credit scores indicate a less risky borrower.

Borrower work status plays a role in the risk evaluation. If the borrower is self-employed, the loan is considered riskier than if the borrower is salaried. Self-employed borrowers tend to have wider fluctuations in cash flow, adding a layer of risk.

The length of the loan term factors into the risk equation since the system considers a 30-year fixed-rate mortgage less risky than an adjustable-rate, while 15-year mortgages are considered less risky than either the 30-year fixed or the adjustable-rate programs.

Statistically, occupancy as a primary residence or second home presents the least amount of risk; whereas investment property represents the highest level of risk.

The mortgage underwriting software takes account of credit and all risk factors to finally stamp the application with an Approve, Refer, or Refer with Caution (not approved) loan status. The object of the game for the borrower is to lower the risk factors presented to the system. If there are high-risk factors to input, look for positive factors that can offset the risk.

Underwriting Overlays

Overlays are extra loan guidelines required by a lender that are stricter than the guidelines required by Fannie Mae and Freddie Mac. Borrowers turned down by one bank based on a lending overlay might get approved with a different one using the same government-backed loan product.

Some banks and mortgage companies have extra regulations that go over and above the normal government loan program regulations. In other words, they ask borrowers to jump through more hoops.

This is what happened to a customer we will call Dave who went to a big bank for a Veterans Administration loan. He had a contract to purchase a home and needed to give notice to his landlord and vacate his rental within a couple of months. His lender granted him a conditional approval, and he sent in all of his documents. The appraisal came back looking good. He was told the loan was approved. The next day he got word from his lender that his loan was denied because he did not have enough money in reserves for emergencies.

The loan officer had correctly informed him that VA did not require reserves at closing. What they did not know was that the *bank* had a regulation overlay that required reserves equal to a certain number of house payments. Dave and his family panicked.

He took his family to a different bank, this time asking up front. That bank did not have the overlay regulation. Dave went with the new bank and had the loan fully approved and ready to close in two weeks. The story ended well with Dave and his family getting to move into their new home on time.

Overlays can trip you up if you do not know about them. Sometimes banks do not publicize their overlays. In this case, the first bank did not even clarify this to their own loan officer. It's not a bad idea to do like Dave did … and ask up front.

Ren

Plan before You Pay

Not long ago, Ren called me and said he was finally ready to buy his first home. He announced: "I am going to use my money to pay off ALL my bills before I come in to see you. Don't you think that is the best thing?"

I suggested, "Before you spend a dime paying anything off, Ren, let's get a snapshot of where you are right now."

Money Talks Loudest

Ren's apartment lease would be up soon and he needed a strong prequalification letter and a quick approval to be in the new house before he had to get out of his apartment. He was worn out with paying rent money every month when he could be investing in his own home. With just enough saved to pay the 3% to 5% down payment on the house he wanted, he was concerned about previously existing debts.

I truly appreciated Ren's willingness to go the extra mile to help me get his loan file looking its best; nevertheless, the top priority with mortgage underwriting is not to eliminate debts but to show adequate cash for down payment and closing costs, and it always looks good to have reserve funds left for emergencies.

Good Credit Can Take You Far

The second important factor in making a borrower like Ren look good is to show a high credit score. Ren had a credit history demonstrating that he pays his creditors on time and stays below 30% credit usage. I pointed out to Ren that his excellent credit score of 780 was well about the average 700. When the borrower's credit score is 650 or 640, then he can probably still get a standard mortgage, but some loan programs will cost more money.

Debt-to-Income Ratios: Can You Make the Payment?

After looking at funds available and the credit profile, underwriters look at debt-to-income ratios. Ren's debt-to-income ratio added the new proposed house payment including PITI and mortgage insurance together with all the minimum payment amounts from credit cards, car loan, and other installment accounts. This total divided into his gross income equals the debt-to-income ratio.

For Ren, his debt-to-income ratio—total monthly debt divided into gross income—was around 45%. Not bad.

In some cases, the mortgage underwriting program could have prequalified Ren with a 50% debt-to-income ratio because he keeps more than enough cash available in his bank account. We also looked at some down payment assistance programs for Ren.

Ren ended up with a strong prequalification letter. He was confident going into the real estate market to purchase his first home.

Once the home appraisal and title work were done, Ren got all of his income and asset supporting documents into the file. Then, a human underwriter reviewed the information and made the ultimate decision. There are three options available to the underwriter: approve the loan; suspend the loan subject to further documentation; or deny the loan. "Approve" is the endgame goal, and I'm glad to say Ren got his win.

CHAPTER 20

How to Avoid or Lessen Mortgage Insurance Costs

Save your money. Saving money is just like earning money.
Idlehearts.com

CAN YOU REMEMBER that confident satisfaction you felt the last time you saved yourself a lot of money? It is a beautiful feeling for this mortgage officer to help a client experience that satisfaction. Saving the mortgage customer by setting up reduced closing costs, a better interest rate, and structuring the loan so the customer pays less for mortgage insurance are all great ways to give the customer that confident, satisfied feeling.

One of the top ways to reduce your mortgage costs is to pay less for private mortgage insurance (PMI). PMI on a conventional mortgage loan does *not* benefit the borrower. Why would you want to pay for something that only benefits the lender?

Private mortgage insurance is not homeowners insurance and it is not credit life insurance. It will not pay the borrower anything, ever. It is required by the lender on conventional mortgages when the borrower pays less than 20% down. The borrower can choose to pay PMI once as a single-pay lump sum; they can pay monthly PMI until the loan balance drops below 78% loan-to-value; or they can pay a portion up front for a smaller monthly payment.

The rate the borrower pays for mortgage insurance varies depending on the loan-to-value, the borrower's credit score, and whether it is a 15-, 20- or 30-year term.

Here are some examples of what the borrower might pay for private mortgage insurance on a $200,000 house with 10% down on a 30-year loan.

Henry Harris

How to Pay Less for a Private Mortgage

Henry Harris is 35 years old, buying his first home for $200,000. In order to keep his payments lower, he agreed to take some money out of savings for a 10% down payment on a 30-year fixed-rate loan. Henry plans to keep the home for five years or less before selling it and moving to a bigger home. Henry tells us his credit score is 760.

A single-pay private mortgage insurance payment for Henry might look something like this:
$1,710 in addition to the $20,000 down payment and closing costs and prepaid taxes and insurance. Since Henry is paying one lump sum, there are no monthly insurance payments.

$200,000 sale price – $20,000 down payment = $180,000 loan amount × .95% PMI = $1,710.

A monthly private mortgage insurance payment for Henry might look something like this:
$200,000 sale price – $20,000 down payment = $180,000 × .25% = $450/12 months = $37.50/month for private mortgage insurance until the loan amount owed is 78% or less of the value of the home.

If the home's value goes up as Henry is paying down the loan balance, he could ask the lender to reappraise the home to determine whether the higher value would advance him to a 78% loan-to-value or better. If he does have a value high enough, and he has paid his mortgage as agreed, the monthly mortgage insurance could be discontinued.

A split private mortgage insurance plan for Henry might look something like this:

A split pay would allow Henry to pay part of the private mortgage insurance in a lump sum once. He would then pay a smaller monthly payment until the home value is 78% or less from what is owed on the loan balance.

$200,000 – 20% down payment = $180,000 loan amount × .50% (PMI factor) = upfront lumpsum $900.

For the monthly PMI payment: $200,000 – 20% down payment = $180,000 loan amount × .25% =$25.50/monthly PMI to be paid until the loan balance is less than 78% of the home value.

The cost of private mortgage insurance is higher if the loan-to-value is higher and if the credit score is lower. Some private mortgage insurance will not cover mortgages if the borrower's monthly debts plus the new house note add up to over 45% of his gross income.

Comparing Private Mortgage Insurance Costs on the Conventional Affordable and Other Special Loan Products

If Henry Harris had chosen to put only 3% instead of 10% as a down payment, then we would have compared a standard conventional program with an Affordable special program. In this case, Henry Harris' income exceeded the maximum household income limit for the geographical area, so he did not qualify for any of the special programs.

If Henry's household income fell within the guidelines set for the area where his new home was located, then he could have paid less for private mortgage insurance than on a standard loan program with only 3% down.

Comparing the Conventional Private Mortgage Insurance to an FHA Loan Program

FHA is a government program that allows the borrower a 3.5% down payment. FHA also charges the borrower an upfront FHA mortgage insurance premium and a monthly mortgage insurance payment. If the borrower puts down 3.5% on a $200,000 30-year FHA loan, the borrower would add 1.75% of the base loan to the total loan amount. Henry would be paying about .85% of the base loan amount monthly for the life of the loan.

$200,000 sale price × 3.5% down payment =$193,000 base loan amount × 1.75% ($196,377 loan amount with upfront mortgage insurance).

$193,000 base loan amount × .85% = $1,641/12 months = $137/month mortgage insurance. This monthly mortgage insurance stays on the loan for the life of the loan, even though the dollar amount reduces as the loan is paid down.

Henry Harris considered ways he could pay less for mortgage insurance. He decided to go with the Conventional purchase loan with 10% down and the monthly mortgage insurance. He felt the value of the property he was buying would continue to go up and he could get rid of the monthly mortgage insurance sooner.

Here's how to get rid of private mortgage insurance:

You must have a good payment track record. Your payments must have been made as agreed. Some companies require that you pay at least 12-24 months on the PMI before requesting to have it removed.

Call your lender. If you already have a conventional mortgage and you think the balance is less than 80% of today's value on your home, you can call your lender and ask them to remove the private mortgage insurance from your payment. They will probably want some money from you to order an appraisal verifying your mortgage is indeed less than 80% of your home's current value and that you have been paying private mortgage insurance on that loan for at least 24 months.

Work with an experienced mortgage officer. Play it smart and save thousands of dollars over time by choosing the right structure on a conventional loan. As a mortgage loan officer, my first job is to make sure I cut the cost of the loan as much as possible. One way to do that is to help buyers avoid paying mortgage insurance. Whether they applied online, by phone, or in-person, I have helped many customers eliminate all or part of what they would have paid in mortgage insurance.

Resources

Radian Private Mortgage Insurance Rate finder

https://www.radian.com/tools-and-technologies/tools/mi-rate-finder

APPENDIX 1

Get-It-Right-the-First-Time Mortgage Program Checklist

(Loan Officer's Name Here)
(Loan Officer's Contact Information)

1. <u>**What is the maximum house payment I can afford right now?**</u>
    A. Several financial gurus say that your total house note, including principal and interest, taxes, homeowners insurance, mortgage insurance, and homeowners association fees should be between 25% and 30% of your gross income. Your total debt-to-income ratios, including the new house payment and payments on other debt, should not exceed 38% to 45% of your gross income. Consult with a certified financial advisor.
    B. Mortgage underwriting software can sometimes approve your debt-to-income ratios at 45% or upwards of 55% of your gross income. Regardless of what the mortgage software tells you, decide on your PERSONAL comfort level and stick to that.
    C. Consider where you plan to be in the next one, five, and ten years.
        Are you planning to retire? If so, what will be your retirement income? Will you be living in the same place?
        Are you planning to get married? Do you plan on expanding your family? Do you plan on taking an aging family member into your home? How much do you estimate your living

expenses may increase? Will your income likely increase, too? If so, by how much?

Are you just getting started in your career? Is it likely your income will go up? Will you need to relocate? How long do you expect to keep the house? What would it cost to rent versus *buy* a home like the one you want?

D. Do you own a house with a lot of equity that you plan on selling within a year of buying the new house? Do you plan to make a large prepayment to the principal once you sell your old home? You might consider a "bridge loan" so you can enjoy the benefits of a much lower payment on your new home without having to immediately sell your old one.

E. Do you plan on starting your own business or acquiring income-producing real estate? This might require you to keep your mortgage payment low so that you can afford to finance other investments.

2. <u>What is the maximum down payment that is comfortable for you?</u>

Several financial gurus say that if you enjoy a stable, salaried job, you probably need about three months of living expenses in an emergency fund. If you are self-employed or get a 100% commission income, you probably need about one full year of living expenses in an emergency fund.

3. <u>What kind of property are you purchasing?</u>

   A. If the property is a fixer-upper with lots of needed repairs, you may want to consider a renovation and repair loan.

   B. Is the property you are purchasing going to be your primary residence, a second home, or a rental property?

   C. Is the property you are financing a condominium or a manufactured home?

   D. Is the property located in a place where special financing is available?

4. <u>What special mortgage programs are available to you?</u>

   A. Are you a military veteran? Are you eligible for the Veteran Administration 100% VA home loan?

   B. Are you a first-time homebuyer, not having your name on the title to real estate within the last 36 months? There may be down payment assistance programs available to you, even if you are not a first-time homebuyer.

5. <u>**What methods can we use to develop more than one exit strategy?**</u>

    A. Is the property in an area that is going up in value? If you needed to sell the home one day, you could probably do it profitably if the value is stable or headed upward.

    B. Is the property in an area that is a strong rental market? In a pinch, you could possibly rent the house and get a nice income from the home.

    C. Is the mortgage you have an assumable loan? If mortgage rates go up, one day someone may be willing to pay you good money to have the opportunity to qualify to assume your low-interest rate mortgage when they buy your home.

Dos and Don'ts for a Smooth Mortgage Process

DURING MY TIME in service as a mortgage loan officer, I've learned that forewarned is forearmed. It is best to set customers' expectations by informing them of what the mortgage industry is expecting from them.

The Dos and Don'ts below is a list I've sent to my mortgage clients from 2018 through 2021. It will be updated as times and loan guidelines change.

Name: (Loan Officer's Name Here)
(Loan Officer's Contact Information)

1) _____(initials) **It is vitally important that you do not change anything on your asset statements after your loan officer has reviewed your bank statements. Any decrease in your assets could make or break your loan approval or cause a delay in your closing. ANY LARGE DEPOSIT NOT PAYROLL RELATED NEEDS TO HAVE THE SOURCE DOCUMENTED. (You can get images of the deposit and copies of deposit slips from your bank.)**

2) _____(initials) **If you are legally married, and buying or refinancing a primary residence, even if your spouse is neither on the loan nor on the title, your spouse will be required to sign a few key documents to keep your title clean under the state law. Change in marital status could cause problems on the title.**

3) _____ (initials) <u>**When it comes time to provide bank statements or any asset account, or tax return, it is necessary to provide ALL pages of the statement, even if it is a blank page. On asset account statements, make sure the name of the bank, your name, and at least part of the account number appear on any bank documentation you submit to us.**</u>

(If you turn in a 401(k) statement, please get a letter from the administrator stating terms of the plan including terms of withdrawal—even if you are not withdrawing funds.)

4) _____ (initials) **Please do not make any changes to your income or manner of payment from income from your business or employment. When it is time to send tax returns, please send ALL pages including any K-1s if applicable. Even if your income is increasing, under current loan guidelines some methods of income payment are not allowed to be counted as qualifying income, so it is important to let your loan officer know of upcoming changes right away, to make sure the type of payment of income is acceptable for loan qualification purposes. If you own 25% or more of a business, please send all pages of the business tax returns for the past 2 years also. (In some cases, underwriting may require a year-to-date Profit and Loss for self-employed borrowers.) Note:** *If your IRS transcripts or tax returns indicate that taxes are owed, you must document the source of funds to clear the taxes owed or show proof of accepted payment plan and proof of three months payments made to IRS or other agency to clear debt.*

(Some mortgage products do not require tax returns at all—check with your mortgage officer for a personalized list of documents needed for your specific loan.)

(Please disclose any payment plans made to IRS or other outside agreements that may not show on the credit report. These payments need to be calcuated to determine your true debt-to-income ratio. Please disclose any IRS or other liens that might show up on other reports connected to you. Not disclosing these can jeapordize your loan approval later in the process.)

5) _____ (initials) **If you file your tax returns right before or during the loan process, this can delay your loan process by a month or more, due to the time it takes the IRS to fully process**

and log your numbers into the government required IRS third-party transcript for that tax return that must be included in your loan file. You may consider filing an extension on filing your IRS return in order to avoid this delay. (Underwriting may ask for a year-to-date Profit and Loss for self-employed borrowers.)

6) _____ (initials) Do not open any new credit accounts (and especially not a 12-months-same-as-cash account.) Do not add balances to any existing credit accounts. Do not apply for any new credit during the loan process. Do not make any changes on your credit status.

7) _____ (initials) Please check your tax returns and make sure you do not have any undisclosed business losses. If you do, please notify your loan officer.

8) _____ (initials) Make sure that you keep your accounts paid current during the loan process. Even though you are planning to pay off an account at closing, please do not allow this account or any others, including any mortgages, to go 30 days late even if the closing is delayed. (This could cause your credit scores to drop right before closing and jeopardize your loan approval.)

9) _____ (initials) Use funds for closing DIRECTLY from the account where we have verified your funds. If funds come from a different account, it can delay or jeopardize your closing. Also do not move money from the account where funds were verified to another account to access for closing. Funds must come DIRECTLY from the account where funds were verified and not moved to a different account for any reason. Earnest money must come from the account that you will be fully documenting.

10)_____(initials) Remember, at closing the funds will need to be in the form of a cashier's check and/or wire payable to the closing agent. You will need 2 forms of ID at closing, including a driver's license. All borrowers and interested parties will need this documentation at closing.

11)_____ (initials) If you are on any of the accounts we are verifying with another person, you will need to get a short letter, dated and signed by the other person identifying the account and stating that you have full access to the funds.

12) _____ (initials) **If there will be a full appraisal on the property you are financing, please inspect the subject property for repairs that may be required prior to closing by the appraiser. Some commonly required repairs are the leaky roof, rotted wood, peeling paint, torn flooring, broken tile, non-functional plumbing, electrical or HVAC systems, drainage problems, holes in sheetrock, broken windows, foundational problems, termite damage, hazardous waste on the property, etc.**

If the property is in a flood zone, flood insurance will be required. Appraisal values are determined by the assigned appraiser. Comparable property sales over the last 6 months to a year on houses like the subject property in the subject property neighborhood are used to determine the official value used by the mortgage company. Government guidelines require the mortgage company to order an appraisal and have the appraiser be assigned to the property by a third-party, government-approved order agency separate from the mortgage company.

The mortgage company must order the appraisal from the approved agency. Appraisals from other mortgage companies and appraisals ordered by anyone else are not qualified to be used under current loan regulations.

If the appraiser notes repairs on the appraisal, it is very possible he/she will need to reinspect the property to make sure repairs are completed in a workmanlike manner. Appraisers charge an extra fee to do this which could increase your costs at closing. Appraisal fees are not refundable.

13) _____ (initials) **If you are refinancing your home, please make sure the home has not been listed for sale on the market within the last 6 months. Remember that on a primary residence, there is a 3 day right of recission before money is disbursed.**

14) _____ (initials) **Due to the new TRID government lending guidelines, there are mandatory delays set up throughout the process, giving you a chance to review the terms as the process moves forward. If you change anything that triggers a change in the final terms after final disclosures have been sent, this could delay your closing to wait on new documents to be received by you and the mandated delay period completed.**

15) _____(initials) **Due to a rising number of incidences of hackers/scammers attempting to redirect wired closing funds, please do NOT have any funds wired before verifying the wiring information with your loan officer and the attorney's office. There may be additional steps to take to ensure your money is wired to the correct account.**

_____   _____

Borrower signature / Date   **Co/Borrower signature / Date**

I, _____, **give permission to my loan officer team to update my realtor(s)/agent(s) with general status on my loan progress.**

_____   _____

Borrower signature/Date   **Co/Borrower signature/Date**

Supporting Documents Commonly Required by the Mortgage Lender

MORTGAGE LOAN PROGRAMS may differ on the types of supporting documents they require. The underwriting software continues to get more sophisticated. If the software retrieves an official verification of employment with details on job and payment history, the borrower may not be required to send employment information; nevertheless, it is better to be prepared with the income documents in case the lender should need them before closing.

Supporting Documents & Funds Required

1. **ALL PAGES of your last two years' tax returns.**
   (If you are self-employed and own over 25% of a business, please include the last two years' corporate or partnership tax returns with all pages including any K-1s. in some cases a year-to-date Profit & Loss statement may be required.)

   If your IRS transcripts or tax returns indicate that taxes are owed, you must document the source of funds to clear the taxes owed or show proof of accepted payment plan and proof of three months' payments made to IRS or other agency to clear debt.

   (Please disclose any payment plans made to IRS or other outside agreements that may not show on the credit report. These

payments need to be calculated to determine your true debt-to-income ratio.)

2. Money for the home appraisal (if needed).
3. ALL W-2s and 1099s that go with the last two years' tax returns plus the W-2s and 1099s received in January of the latest year
4. Latest paystubs (2).
5. ALL PAGES of the last two months' bank statements and investment accounts.
6. Legible copy of your driver's license(s).
7. Name and contact info for your chosen homeowners insurance agency that will cover the financed property.
8. A signed and dated letter explaining the status on any inquiries appearing on the credit report to state whether a new account was opened or not. If a new account was opened as a result of an inquiry on the credit report, all pages of the latest statement for that account must be submitted.
9. Divorce decree and marital dissolution agreement/child support documentation if applicable.

If you receive retirement income:

10. Submit all pages of the latest entitlement letter from social security or other pension or retirement fund.

If you own rental real estate property or any other real estate property:

11. All pages of leases on properties
12. A declaration page from your insurance company on each property verifying the coverage, premium amount, next due date, and if there are any liens on the property.
13. Copy of municipal/county tax record showing the amount of property taxes levied to each rental property.
14. Verification of association fees if any on any of the rental properties.
15. Latest mortgage statements on each applicable property.

16. All pages of closing disclosures showing the sale or purchase of any real estate properties that transferred after the last tax year reported.

If you are getting any kind of down payment assistance, you will most likely need to successfully complete a HUD-approved Homebuyers Education Course. We suggest United Housing in Memphis (901) 272-1122, but there are others available. If you need this class, please set up as early as possible to complete it.

If you are an active-duty military veteran, in reserves, or discharged and you are applying for a VA mortgage, please include a copy of your DD214. If you have an updated Certificate of Entitlement, please send that, too.

In case you are refinancing a home:

17. Include a copy of the latest three mortgage statements or lien statements secured on that property.

18. Make sure your home has not been listed for sale within the last six months.

APPENDICES 4-5, 7-11

Appendix 4: Calculating Principal & Interest Payments

Appendix 5: Top Things To Know About A Residential Real Estate Appraisal

Appendix 7: Good Things to Know When You Are Going to Buy a Home

Appendix 8: Good Things to Know about Selling a Home

Appendix 9: Good Things to Know When You Are Facing Foreclosure

Appendix 10: Good Things to Know about a Home Inspection

Appendix 11: Good Things to Know about a Real Estate Closing

ALL OF THESE appendices can be downloaded at:
https://jogarner.com/best-mortgage-book/downloads-for-book-owners/

APPENDIX 6

Dealing with Divorce and Your Mortgage

IF IT IS clear that you will be required to refinance your existing mortgage and pay off your ex-spouse to get them off the loan, **it is easier to get approved and closed on a mortgage BEFORE you file divorce rather than during the divorce procedure. It can also work smoother AFTER the final divorce decree has been recorded.**

If you are planning to buy a new home or refinance your home, remember that most of your standard mortgage programs will not accept child support, alimony, or separate maintenance income unless the marital dissolution agreement shows that you will be entitled to this income for at least 36 months **from the date of your home loan CLOSING.** If you are the person that will be receiving child support, alimony or separate maintenance, consider negotiating to get this income for more than five years and not less.

- Credit—Get your name off any accounts that are under the control of your spouse. Even if the divorce agreement orders the other party to pay designated bills, if they don't pay and your name is on the account, you are responsible to pay the creditor. If you don't, your credit will be damaged.
- Make your payments on time.
- Keep your credit card debt under 30% usage. This can help you boost your credit scores.

Real Estate and Business Solutions for Making a Fresh Start Dealing with Divorce

Joseph Jefford

"I love my kids. I want a house that I can make a home where they will love to come to spend time with their dad."

The one thing Joseph Jeffords loved more than life was his two elementary school-age sons, Jimmy and Jack. Joseph tried everything to keep his family together, but his wife wanted a divorce and she wanted full custody of their two sons.

Joseph was heartbroken and financially hurting, too. His credit was messed up from some jointly held bills his ex-wife was responsible to pay...but didn't. The creditors came after Joseph. Nothing seemed fair.

Joseph worked two jobs, paid more legal fees, and fought to keep custody of his children. Nothing seemed to work, but he sought wisdom from reputable professionals. After several attempts, the agreement finally allowed his boys to stay with him every other weekend and alternating holidays.

It took Joseph about a year to get his credit cleaned up and restore his emergency savings. When he came to get preapproved for his mortgage, he said, "I love my kids. I want a house that I can make a home where they will love to come to spend time with their dad."

Joseph put a good realtor on his team and got his home with a low, affordable payment and small down payment. The low house payment made the treehouse and other fun times with his children affordable. The low money down left him with his emergency fund and a lot of peace of mind.

Carley Clemmons

Rising from the Ashes Following Divorce

Carley found herself in what felt like the ash heap of life following some grueling years going through a divorce. She had to build back her credit...and her self-confidence.

Divorce can be truly devastating—not just financially but emotionally as it affects many aspects of how people see life. Carley had been married for many years, and she and her ex-husband had always owned their own home. After the divorce, she had to sell the house and go back to renting.

Carley had to make a choice. She could give in and let resentment and negative events crush her into the dust, or she could choose to rise from the ashes and create a quality life as a better person. Carley chose to reinvent herself and recreate a life she would love while helping others in the process. A big part of living out this dream was to own her own home again. Carly would make the home her castle and security blanket—complete with a she-shed out back to enjoy her hobbies.

It took over three years to build back her credit, pay off old bills, and reinvent herself as a person. She found a house that she loved but lacked funds to pay for the down payment and other costs. Down Payment Assistance enabled her to buy the house she wanted in the area where she wanted to live. It was ultimately the right down payment assistance program that handed her the final "keys" to start her new life.

Resources

Real Estate and Business Solutions for Making a Fresh Start Dealing with Divorce (from panel of professionals on Real Estate Mortgage Shoppe radio show) https://jogarner.com/real-estate-and-business-solutions-for-making-a-fresh-start-dealing-with-divorce/

Good Things to Know about Home Insurance

*Content comes from Real Estate Mortgage Shoppe
professional insurance guests*

1. **Talk about some of the common ways you save your customers money on their homeowners' insurance.** Bundling and finding multiple opportunities to add discounts to the plans. The more coverage you have with an insurance company, the more discounts on your premiums you can enjoy. Also, when you have claims, the insurance company is less likely to drop your insurance coverage because you have multiple types of coverage with them.

2. **What is bundling? What kind of difference can bundling insurance coverage make on the overall price of insurance?** Bundling is when you buy multiple types of insurance coverages from the same insurance company. Typical insurance policies to bundle include homeowners insurance, auto insurance, umbrella policies, and life insurance policies. In many cases bundling the home insurance and auto insurance can save you 10% to 20% on the cost of the overall coverage for qualified customers. Shop the cost of insurance coverage with different insurance companies because one company may offer a bargain price on auto insurance but charge more on the homeowner insurance policy.

3. **What are the benefits of renters insurance for the tenant and the landlord?** Renters insurance is the best insurance a landlord will never have to pay. Many landlords require their tenants to have renters insurance to cover incidents caused by the renter or simply to cover the renters' belongings in case of fire or other hazards. Renters insurance is good for the tenant because it helps them get a good price on homeowners insurance when it comes time for them to buy.

4. **What about life insurance? What is the best way to buy life insurance?** There are two basic types of policies—term life and whole life. Term life is very popular with younger people who need more coverage due to having dependent children and a bigger mortgage, etc. Whole life policies provide lifelong coverage with premiums that do not go up. Here are three guarantees from most whole life policies:
    - A guaranteed minimum rate of return on the cash value.
    - The promise that your premium payments won't go up.
    - A guaranteed death benefit that won't go down.

5. **What about an umbrella policy? What does it cover? How much does it cost?** The umbrella policy protects you over and above what your regular policy does not cover. For instance, if you have a $1,000,000 umbrella policy, you may be able to save a lot more money on your regular homeowner's policy and car insurance because you can buy coverage with a larger deductible, making those policies a lot less expensive. In case of an incident, the umbrella can pick up what the other policy does not cover. Using the combination of regular homeowners and car insurance with the lower-priced higher deductibles saves you enough money to easily pay the umbrella policy.

6. **When do you need a vacant house policy? What risk do you take if you do not have vacant house insurance when your house is vacant?** If your home will be vacant for 60 days or more, you need a vacant home policy. If you have a claim and the home has been

vacant 60 days without a vacant home policy, then you risk not being covered at all.

7. **What to DO and NOT DO when it comes to buying your insurance and filing a claim?** DO NOT call the 1-800 number when you are asking about a claim. In many cases, even if no claim is paid or needed, it can still show up as a mark against your record as if you actually filed a claim. DO call your personal insurance agent to inquire about whether you should file a claim. Your insurance agent can help keep your record clean if there is no reason to actually file a claim.

If You're a Fan of This Book, Please Tell Others...

- Post a 5-Star review on Amazon.

- Write about the book on your Facebook, Twitter, Instagram page—any social media you regularly use! #ChoosingTheBestMortgage

- If you blog, consider referencing the book, your study experiences, or publishing an excerpt from the book with a link to my website. You have my permission to do this as long as you provide proper credit and backlinks.

- Recommend the book to friends. Word-of-mouth is still the most effective form of advertising.

- Purchase additional copies to give as gifts. You can do this by visiting my website: jogarner.com

Glossary

3-1 ARM A hybrid adjustable-rate mortgage with an interest rate initially fixed for three years then adjusts each year.

5-1 ARM A hybrid adjustable-rate mortgage with an interest rate initially fixed for five years then adjusts each year.

12-Months-Same-as-Cash allows the borrower 12 months of no payments. After 12 months, the borrower is required to pay back the principal with interest on a monthly basis.

Adjustable-Rate Mortgage (ARM) A loan characterized by a fluctuating interest rate, usually tied to a specified index.

Amortized Loan A loan in which the principal and interest are payable in monthly or other periodic installments over the term of the loan.

Annual Percentage Rate (APR) The relationship of the total finance charges associated with the loan. Calculation disclosing financing costs including rate, points, and other fees charged by the lender.

Appraisal An estimate of value on a piece of real estate performed by a professional appraiser.

Appraisal Management Company (AMC) is an independent entity through which mortgage lenders order residential real estate valuation services. AMCs assign the appraiser to each order, review, and send the appraisal to the lender.

Acquisition Cost is the total cost to purchase a real estate property including the cost of the property, appraisal fees, attorney fees, credit report, hazard insurance, and loan fees.

Assumption is the act of taking over mortgage payments from a previous borrower. Most assumable loans require the person assuming the mortgage to qualify through the mortgage company servicing the loan at the time of the assumption.

Automated Underwriting Software Software programs for underwriting mortgage programs on loans to be sold in the secondary market.

Berm Home Built above grade or partially below grade, with earth covering one or more walls.

Bracketing is a process in which the appraiser determines a probable range of values for a property by applying qualitative techniques of comparative analysis to a group of comparable sales.

Buydown Extra points paid to obtain a lower than the market interest rate.

Cash Out Refinance Cash out refinancing occurs when a mortgage is taken out on a property already owned. The new loan amount is above and beyond the cost of the transaction, payoff of existing liens, and related expenses.

Census Tract is an area roughly equivalent to a neighborhood established by the Bureau of Census for analyzing populations.

Certificate of Eligibility Issued by VA stating amount of entitlement available to the veteran to qualify for no-money-down VA loan.

Closing Cost Costs from title companies, the mortgage company, and other third party fees when purchasing or refinancing real estate.

Closing Disclosure is a form that a lender provides to a borrower at least three business days before the loan closes. The disclosure outlines the final terms and costs of the mortgage.

Collateral That which protects the rights of a lender in case of default on a loan.

Compensating Factors Positive features that may offset negatives, increasing the possibility for approval of the borrower's loan application.

Comparable Sales are a list of recent home sales that reflect the characteristics of the home an owner is looking to sell.

Condominium Form of ownership granting fee simple title to an owner, plus an undivided interest in the common areas.

Conforming Loan A mortgage meeting the Fannie Mae/Freddie Mac guidelines.

Construction Loan Made for the purpose of constructing houses or other buildings. Funds are generally dispersed in increments called "draws" as various stages of construction are completed.

Cost of Funds Index commonly used for adjustable-rate mortgages based on the average costs of borrowed funds by depository institutions.

Credit Inquiry is a request from an institution for a credit report on a consumer from a credit reporting agency.

Department of Housing & Urban Development (HUD) The United States Department of Housing and Urban Development is a cabinet department in the executive branch of the U.S. federal government.

Department of Veterans Affairs (DVA) The United States Department of Veterans Affairs is a federal Cabinet-level agency that provides integrated services to veterans, including home loans.

Discount Point Charged by the lender to buy the interest rate below the going market rate. One discount point equals one percent of the loan amount.

Down Payment The difference between the sales price and the loan amount paid by purchaser.

Draw Period is the amount of time the borrower can withdraw funds from a home equity line of credit. After the draw period ends, the borrower must repay the loan.

Earnest Money Earnest money is a deposit the buyer pays in good faith to the seller to buy a home.

Equity is the net value of an asset—the difference between the property's present value and the amount still owed on the mortgage.

Equity Line of Credit A home equity line of credit allows homeowners to borrow money against the equity they have in their home and receive that money as a line of credit.

Escrow Account Money held by a third party on behalf of others.

Fannie Mae Federal National Mortgage Association

FICO Score is a three-digit number based on the information in your credit reports. Fair Isaac Corporation generates these number scores based on account information reported to the bureaus by the borrowers' creditors.

Freddie Mac Federal Home Loan Mortgage Corporation

FHA Federal Housing Administration

Foreclosure The legal process whereby lender receives title to real estate property with the right to sell the property and repay the mortgage lien.

Fully Documented A mortgage program that requires the borrower to supply income, asset and credit supporting documents to be reviewed for qualification.

Funding Fee Percentage of loan amount charged on VA loans to provide a pool of funds for administrative costs.

Geodesic Home Almost spherical shape based on a geodesic polyhedron. Because of their curved walls and ceiling, these domes use approximately a third less surface area to enclose the same volume as a traditional box home.

Guarantee A loan that is guaranteed by a government agency, which will purchase the debt from the lending financial institution and take on responsibility for the loan if the borrower defaults.

Homeowners insurance Insurance carried by the homeowner to protect the dwelling in case of fire and other hazards.

Housing Ratio is the ratio between house payment (including the principal and interest, taxes, insurance, mortgage insurance and association fee) and the monthly gross income.

Index Financial indicator used as a basis to calculate ARM rate.

Interest-only Home Equity Line of Credit allows the borrower to borrow money, repay it, and borrow again as needed during the draw period. During that time of revolving access to cash, only the interest is due until the draw period has ended.

Interest Rate Cap Established by lender providing protection for borrower that interest rate cannot exceed stated limits.

Jumbo Loan Any mortgage loan exceeding the Fannie Mae/Freddie Mac conforming maximum loan limit.

Lender Premium when the borrower locks in a mortgage rate that is higher than the market rate in exchange for getting a credit from the lender to apply toward paying closing costs.

Lien A financial claim against the property.

Lifetime Cap The maximum increase in interest rate allowed over the life of the loan.

Loan-to-Value (LTV) Loan amount shown as a percentage of the property's value. The ratio between the loan amount and purchase price of the home. Lenders determine loan-to-value on the lesser of the value or purchase price.

Manufactured Home is a prefabricated home formerly known as a mobile home. They are assembled in a factory and shipped to the site.

Margin The amount added to the index to determine the rate on an adjustable-rate mortgage.

Mortgage Lender of money secured by real estate.

Mortgage-Backed Securities Income-producing securities based on mortgage loan packages.

Mortgage Insurance Insurance protecting the lender against the default by the borrower.

Mortgage Insurance Premium (MIP) Mortgage insurance charged on FHA loans. FHA has an upfront mortgage insurance premium added to the top of the base loan amount. FHA also has a monthly mortgage insurance program.

Non-Conforming Loan A loan that does not follow Fannie Mae or Freddie Mac conforming guidelines.

No-Start Letter is a letter the construction loan lender gives to indicate there are no liens secured on the property where construction is about to begin. No commencement of construction can begin until after the closing and recording of the deed of trust to ensure that the lender has priority over any potential lien claims of contractors. This rule is state-specific.

One-Time-Close-Construction-To-Permanent Loan allows the borrower to close one time on a permanent loan taken in draws during the home construction. After the home is completed, payments are made that include both principal and interest and are paid like this until the mortgage is paid off.

Option Period provides the tenant the right to purchase the property at an agreed price during the lease term or other specified term in exchange for a fee paid to the seller. The fee paid is called the "Option Fee."

Origination Fee A charge by the lender for costs of originating mortgage.

Overlays are additional mortgage requirements some lenders require beyond those of the minimum mortgage guidelines.

Paper Losses Also known as non-cash expenses.

PITI Principal, interest, taxes, and insurance on a monthly mortgage payment.

Points The lender charges this to buy the interest rate down below the going market rate.

Private Mortgage Insurance (PMI) Mortgage insurance purchased by the borrower to insure the lender in case of loan default on a loan when the loan amount is more than 80% loan-to-value. Lenders can price the loan differently to the borrower and offer a lender-paid private mortgage insurance program.

Repair Allowance is reimbursement by the seller for repairs such as replacing carpet, paint, and other repairs. Mortgage companies typically do not allow repair allowances because it is cashback to the buyer from the seller. The amount of the allowance adjusts the LTV percentage, meaning the borrower brings more money to closing.

Qualified Income A stable, recurring income type that is acceptable with the loan program being used by the borrower.

Piggyback Second Mortgage A piggyback mortgage is an additional mortgage or loan beyond a borrower's first mortgage loan, which is secured with the same collateral. They are used together to purchase a home.

Purchase-Money-Mortgage This type of mortgage usually replaces part or all of the cash that the buyer would otherwise pay the seller.

Rate Caps *Initial adjustment cap* This cap determines how much the interest rate can increase the first time it adjusts after the fixed-rate period expires. *Subsequent adjustment cap* This cap determines how much the interest rate can increase in the adjustment periods that follow. *Lifetime adjustment cap* This cap says how much the interest rate can increase in total, over the life of the loan.

Recapture Tax applies to borrowers who buy their homes using a government bond program. The recapture tax requires some mortgagors to repay the government a portion of their gain upon sale of the home if they financed their home with a Mortgage Revenue Bond (MRB) loan.

Recapture Time Calculation of the time it will take the savings on a mortgage refinance to replace the cost to refinance.

Recast To redesign an existing loan balance by paying it down over twenty percent. The payments are reduced and amortized to be paid back over the remaining term of the mortgage.

Recording The formal filing of documents affecting a property's title.

Refinance To a get a new mortgage to replace an existing loan or finance a home already owned by the borrower that has no loan on it.

Residual Income The Veteran Home Loan program uses a formula to determine the borrower's discretionary income. This formula factors the number of dependents in the household, maintenance cost of the size of the home, and more.

Seasoning Time Seasoning in real estate usually refers to the length of time that a homeowner has owned a particular home. Lenders put seasoning requirements on refinance loans that require the original loan to be held for a certain amount of time prior to refinancing.

Secondary Market Source that buys mortgages from mortgage companies that originate the loans.

Short Sale in real estate is when a financially distressed homeowner sells their property for less than the amount due on the mortgage.

Specific Power of Attorney grants only certain, tightly defined powers to the attorney-in-fact. This type of power of attorney can be given to someone to sign at a real estate closing on behalf of the person who signed the specific power of attorney.

Subordinate Financing A loan secured on real estate that ranks in a position behind a first mortgage lien.

Targeted Area An economically distressed area designated by the U.S. Department of Housing and Urban Development (HUD).

Title Ownership record of property.

Title insurance Protects the lender and new owner against title defects.

Title Search Conducted by a study of court records to verify seller has clear title to property.

Tradeline is data reported by the creditors to the credit bureaus. This data contains information such as account balances, payment amounts, and payment history on the borrower on a credit account.

Variable Rate A loan characterized by a fluctuating interest rate, usually one tied to a specified index.

Underwriter Person responsible for evaluating the default risk of the applicant for a mortgage loan. Grants approval or denial of the loan.

USDA 100% Loan A low-interest, fixed rate mortgage with a zero down payment for home buyers purchasing in less populated areas.